OLD MAN PREACHER
WILLINGHAM

By the same authors

Now I Know His Name

OLD MAN PREACHER
WILLINGHAM

His Life and Legacy

Frankie Willingham Wyatt

Margaret Sorensen

Edited by
Deborah A. Wyatt Braboy, PhD

TABLELAND PRESS

Published in the USA by

TABLELAND PRESS, LLC
www.tablelandpress.com

ISBN: 978-1-949323-00-9 (paperback)
ISBN: 978-1-949323-01-6 (ebook)

Unless otherwise indicated, all Scripture quotations are taken from the
King James Version of the Holy Bible.

Scripture quotations marked NASB are taken from the New American
Standard Bible®, Copyright © 1960, 1962, 1963, 1968, 1971, 1972, 1973,
1975, 1977, 1995 by The Lockman Foundation. Used by permission.

Printed in the United States of America

To my father,
Wesley Frank Willingham

CONTENTS

PREFACE

This book was written to honor my father, Wesley Frank Willingham. A year before he passed away, I went to my parent's home, with my daughter Carol and son, Jerry, so they could hear Daddy tell the stories of his life. I tape-recorded him sharing the struggles he went through during his early years. Before we left, I asked Daddy to continue to document his memories.

In collecting information for this book, I asked my family for memories they wanted to share. My sister Rowina Lee (Sissy) found a two-page written note with additional information about Daddy's life as well as some of his sermon notes and two tapes of Daddy's sermons. My brother, Jim Willingham, contributed stories. Many other family members have helped and provided information and stories. I am so appreciative and thankful for all their help.

I have also done a lot of research on ancestry.com with help from a friend. Through this search I became friends on Facebook with Karon Hurst Michael, who is one of the great granddaughters of my father's sister Rosa. Karon has done a lot of research on ancestry.com and was able to get in touch with William Midget's great grandson, who gave Karon information regarding William's history. William was one of my father's brothers.

This is Daddy's story. I pray you will be blessed as you see how he always followed God's will for his life and his family. He loved his family, and his desire was for all of his descendants to know and follow Jesus as Savior. Daddy wasn't perfect; he made mistakes, but he lived as godly a life as one could in this fallen world.

Much prayer and research has gone into writing his story. I pray for God's blessings on all who read this book.

— Frankie L. Willingham Wyatt

It has been my joy and privilege to help Frankie write this biography of her father, Wesley Frank Willingham. Learning about his life and testimony for God makes me truly wish that I had known him. To know what he endured in his childhood and to see how God transformed his life is a testament to God's power and glory. This is a very remarkable story, and I am sure that you will be blessed by it.

— Margaret Sorensen

CHAPTER 1

WILLINGHAM HISTORY

Sometimes in life, truth is stranger than fiction. This is the story of Wesley Frank Willingham, an extraordinary man who introduced himself as "Old Man Preacher Willingham." He overcame unimaginable trauma and abuse; yet he unconditionally loved his life, his family, his friends, and, more importantly, his God. For someone lacking a formal education, he had a lot of wisdom—godly wisdom. Wesley's story is inconceivable, which speaks of the goodness and grace of a loving Heavenly Father.

*   *   *

One afternoon in 1914, Wesley Frank Willingham, who was about twelve years old (he wasn't sure because he didn't know his exact birthdate), was taking care of the Gateses' children. All of a sudden, Mrs. Gates came in and started screaming at him. For some reason, she wrongly presumed an offense against her kids. She got the strap and started beating Wesley in front of her children, who cowered in the corner with their hands over their faces. Mrs. Gates's anger just exploded, and she would not stop flogging him. Over and over, the strap cut into his flesh. Wesley had no idea what he had done to receive such a harsh and severe beating. The wounds were very deep, and blood ran down his back. Mrs. Gates didn't stop until she was exhausted and had expended her anger. Wesley could hardly move, but he was still forced to do his outside chores. As Wesley limped out to the barn, he said to himself, *I will never allow the Gateses to beat me again.* So that night when everyone was asleep, he quietly slipped out of the house and, by the light of the moon, made his way to the property of Jim Young. The runaway entered the barn, slowly climbed up into the loft, and covered himself with hay. Wesley planned to get up early the next morning and leave the area before anyone was awake. The straw irritated the cuts on his back, making it difficult for him to get to sleep. But Wesley was so exhausted that he eventually drifted into a deep, sound sleep.

*   *   *

Wesley's father, William Frank Willingham, was born in Montague, Texas, on January 19, 1860. William Frank's father, John Willingham, was born in 1831 in Audrain County, Missouri. His mother, Nancy, was born about 1839 in Missouri. John Willingham had a farm in Montague, and William Frank helped his father with the chores. When his father died in 1882, William Frank continued to work the family farm.

After the American Civil War, cattle became a big industry in Texas. As William Frank was growing up, he often watched the cowboys driving their cattle along the Chisholm Trail, which passed through Montague. The Chisholm Trail (named for its creator, Jesse Chisholm) started in San Antonio, Texas, and ended in Abilene, Kansas. Cattle would be driven along the trail to market in Kansas where they would then be shipped by railroad eastward.

William Frank Willingham.

At the age of twenty, William Frank married Isabell McDonald, who was nineteen years old. Their son, Lee, was born September 24, 1883. Sadly, Isabell died a few years after Lee's birth. William Frank married again and had two daughters: Lizzie (born August 1891) and Maude (born 1894). After the passing of his second wife, William Frank was left with the difficult task of raising his children alone.

*   *   *

Wesley's mother was Martha Luella Hooker, who was born in Missouri about 1873. Her parents were Archibald and Margaret Hooker. Tragically, her father passed away before Luella turned seven.

Prior to meeting William Frank, Luella had married Frank Midget on January 31, 1889 in Lawrence County, Arkansas. Their marriage certificate states that she was only fourteen years old. Her brother John Hooker (born in 1861), who was twelve years older than Luella, signed as security for the one hundred dollar marriage license. Frank and Luella had six children, but only three of them lived: William, Rosa Ann, and Cora. Some time later Frank Midget died, leaving Luella alone to raise their children. Shortly thereafter Luella and the children went to live with her brother John in Lawrence County, Arkansas. John Hooker (whose wife's name was Lila) was a minister as well as a doctor and schoolteacher.

* * *

Meanwhile, William Frank left his three children (Lee, age sixteen; Lizzie, age eight; and Maude, age five) with nearby relatives and went to Lawrence County, Arkansas. The reason for the trip is unknown; it may have been business. It is also unknown how and where Luella and William Frank met, but somehow they became acquainted, and she accepted his proposal of marriage.

William Frank and Luella married toward the end of 1899 in Lawrence County, Arkansas. Her brother John officiated the wedding. Since the winter was beginning to set in, John agreed to take Luella and her children (William, age ten; Rosa Ann, age seven; and Cora, age three) to Texas in a wagon so they could travel at a slower pace, while William Frank rode his horse back to his farm and children.

CHAPTER 2

DIFFICULT TIMES

For John, Luella, and the children, the journey to Texas (which was over five hundred miles) was long and tiring. The wheels of the wagon followed the ruts in the dirt road. Sometimes when it rained or snowed, the wagon would bog down in the mud. Then Luella and the children would get down and wait while John worked to get it moving again.

After a few weeks, they arrived in the Chickasaw Nation territory (present-day Oklahoma), where they stayed with relatives until springtime. While they were there, little Cora became quite ill. John and Luella cared for her as best they could, but Cora's health continued to decline, and she unexpectedly passed away. She was only three years old and had a sweet disposition. Luella found it difficult to watch the life leave the body of her precious Cora; she would miss seeing her run and play. Luella was devastated by the loss, yet she had to pick herself up and continue on. After all, she still had William and Rosa to care for.

With spring rapidly approaching, they continued their journey to Texas. For Luella and the children, the anticipation of meeting their new family was exciting, and yet they were a little nervous.

* * *

Growing up on a farm had taught William Frank the value of hard work. Farming requires long hours every day, working from daylight until dark. Animals have to be cared for the first thing every morning and the last thing every evening. William Frank's morning chores consisted of feeding and milking the cows, feeding the chickens, collecting the eggs, and then feeding the other animals. In the spring, he would go to the barn and hitch the mule to the plow. After preparing the fields, he planted the crops. In the fall, harvesttime was very tedious. Gathering the crops and picking cotton were physically demanding.

Every Monday, using the lye soap that she had made, Luella did the laundry outside on a washboard in a large tub. After the clothes were washed, she hung them on the line to dry. Her daily tasks included cleaning, dusting, and scrubbing the floors. Each day Luella went out to the garden and picked enough vegetables for the day's meals. At noontime, she prepared dinner to take out to William Frank and the men who were helping him in the fields. After a long day, she cooked the evening meal and then rang the bell for the men to come in for supper. Water, which had to be pumped at the kitchen sink into a teakettle or pan, was heated on a wood stove. During wintertime, wood was needed for the potbellied stove in the middle of the living room to heat their home.

*   *   *

During the first couple of years of their marriage, Luella suffered two miscarriages. After becoming pregnant a third time, she started having complications requiring medical attention unavailable to her on the Texas prairie. She and William Frank discussed the possibility of her going back to Arkansas to stay with her brother John. They decided that Luella would have a better chance of delivering a healthy baby if she were staying with her brother and receiving his constant medical care.

William Frank loaded their wagon with clothes, blankets, food, and cooking implements for the long journey. After saying goodbye to his children (who would be taking care of the farm in his absence), William Frank settled Luella, William, and Rosa Ann comfortably in the back of the wagon. He climbed up on the buckboard and clucked to the horses. Clouds of dust rose as they slowly traveled along the dirt road, stopping often for Luella.

A feeling of relief washed over them once they arrived at John and Lila's home in Atkins, Arkansas, and they gave thanks to God for their safe trip. William Frank wished that he could stay and help take care of his wife, but he knew that he needed to get back to the farm and his children. After a couple of days rest, William asked John to take good care of Luella, William, and Rosa Ann, and then headed home. He planned to return for them after the birth of the baby.

*   *   *

On August 12, 1902, Wesley Frank Willingham was born. He was a beautiful, healthy baby boy, and Luella's heart overflowed with happiness. John sent William

Frank a telegram announcing the birth. Everything appeared to be well.

As Luella lay on the bed, holding Wesley, she thought about her husband who was home in Texas. He would be so proud. She remembered the first time she had seen him — how handsome he had looked in his ten-gallon hat. He was big and strong from working on the family farm. She missed her life in Texas and longed to return to her husband and his children.

Wesley's crying brought Luella back to the present. She did the best she could to feed and care for him, but Luella could feel her strength slowly fading.

William and Rosa came in to admire their new baby brother. He was very cute, and they enjoyed watching him sleep.

As the days slowly passed, Luella became concerned and very discouraged because she couldn't regain her strength, as she had after the birth of her previous babies. She was unable to get up and care for Wesley, so she depended a lot on Lila's assistance in caring for herself and her newborn. Each day Luella's body weakened more than the previous day. She knew that there was something very seriously wrong. Sadly, nine days after Wesley's birth, Luella passed away.

CHAPTER 3

KIDNAPPED

Wesley's Uncle John and Aunt Lila, who were both in their forties, had no children of their own. With the death of John's sister, they saw this as an opportunity to have what they had always wanted: a baby. They decided they would keep Wesley and raise him as their own. Therefore, John wired a second telegram to William Frank stating that both Luella and their newborn son had died.

William and Rosa Ann were now orphaned. Having been very young when their father passed away, they now were in shock and grieving over their mother's death. Their world had just been shattered, and they had no idea of what to expect in the coming days. William and Rosa Ann hoped to be reunited with William Frank when he would surely come to get Wesley.

Inexplicably, John and Lila didn't keep Rosa Ann or William. Perhaps the Hookers thought if they kept the older children, it would be easier for William Frank to track them down. Also, if they were found, the children could have told what had happened. Instead,

John—apparently insensitive to the children's grief—sold Rosa Ann as a maid to a wealthy family, and he left William at an orphanage. William was badly mistreated at the orphanage and eventually ran away.

John knew that he would have to move and hide in order to keep and raise Wesley, so to preclude any possibility of being traced, he and Lila promptly moved with Wesley to an isolated, rural area of Arkansas.

When William Frank received the news of his wife's and son's deaths, shock gripped his body. He could not accept that his son was deceased. Something inside of him told him that Wesley was alive.

William Frank immediately sought God's guidance and made plans to look for Wesley. He prayed with his children before leaving to search for their baby brother, asking for God's protection for his children and for safe travels for himself. Packing up a few supplies and his bedroll, he mounted his best horse and headed back to Arkansas to find his son and bring him home. After several long weeks of travel, he arrived at his brother-in-law's house and found someone else living there. He asked around for John Hooker, and the local people informed him that the Hookers had suddenly moved away, without telling anyone where they were going.

This became the pattern for the Hookers. Whenever they heard that William Frank was in the area, they packed up and left. They were always on the move, always having to hide. The Hookers moved from one rural area to another in the Ozarks of Arkansas and Missouri. By the time Wesley was three years old, they were living in Dora, Missouri. John Hooker regularly told Wesley that his father was a very cruel man and that if he ever found him, he would take him away and be mean to him.

* * *

When Wesley was about four years old, his uncle was working at a sawmill in Greenville, Missouri. One day John ran into the house, grabbed Wesley, yelled for Lila to follow him, and hurried out to the barn. He took Wesley up into the loft and hid him among the bales of hay. Then he and Lila quickly put blankets on all the windows, pushed the wooden bolt to secure the barn doors, and joined Wesley in the loft. Wesley knew that his father was looking for him. From the things that his uncle had told him, Wesley was scared to death that William Frank would find him. He didn't want to be taken away from Uncle John and Aunt Lila.

As John, Lila, and Wesley lay quietly in the barn loft, time seemed to stop. While waiting, they listened to the sounds of the horses stomping and nickering. After about an hour, no one tried to enter, so John cautiously peeked out the windows. Seeing no one, he called to Lila and Wesley that the coast was clear.

It wasn't long after this incident that Lila passed away, and it was just Wesley and his uncle moving from place to place, always hiding from Wesley's father. John was able to stay one step ahead of William Frank.

* * *

John often took his doctor's pay in vegetables, eggs, chickens, or whatever the farmers had to share. He also served as a teacher occasionally in the one-room schoolhouse and preached regularly in that same building, which became the church on Sunday. Additionally, he took any odd job that he could find to provide for himself and Wesley.

As Wesley grew older, John taught him his ABC's and numbers, but his uncle never sent him to school. Wesley knew that his name was Wesley Frank Willingham and that he was named after his father. John also told him that his mother had died when he was nine days old. Wesley knew that Uncle John was his mother's older brother and that he and Aunt Lila had no children of their own. Wesley was told that he had siblings on his father's side living in west Texas and that he had a brother, William, and sister, Rosa, on his mother's side.

Always on the run, John and Wesley continued to move around northern Arkansas and southern Missouri. They stayed with various people and lived near Cabool and Willow Springs, Missouri, for a while. They moved to O'Kean, Arkansas, where John agreed to be a share-cropper. Even though John Hooker continued to move from place to place, William Frank never stopped looking for his son.

* * *

When Wesley was about six years old, he and his uncle were living in the countryside close to Risco, Missouri. For years John had been suffering from rheumatism, and his knees were very swollen. However, being a doctor (and also on the run), John thought that he could treat himself. However, he became very sick and ended up bedridden (Wesley tried to keep him as comfortable as he could). Wesley ate whatever he could find in the house and tried to get his uncle to eat, to no avail.

Wesley did all the household chores. He fed the horses and took care of the other animals. Their house was isolated in the country with no close neighbors. Uncle John told Wesley that when they ran out of food, to walk through the woods and look for someone who was squirrel hunting. That person might give them some food.

It was a daily challenge just to figure out what to eat. Each day, Wesley foraged around to find anything edible. Finally, he ate all that was left in the house: a cold biscuit and black pepper. Wesley didn't want to leave his uncle so he stayed with him. On the third day without food, he finally decided that he had to find something to eat or he would starve to death. His uncle seemed to be sleeping peacefully, so Wesley didn't disturb him. Responding to the hunger gnawing in his belly, Wesley left the house.

CHAPTER 4

ABUSED

The sun was rising as Wesley quietly tiptoed off the front porch. He followed a dirt trail that led through the woods. After walking for a while, Wesley came to a fork in the trail. He stood there, not sure which way to turn. He looked down each path as far as he could see, but neither one gave any indication that it would be the right one to take. Which way should he go? Right? Left? Which one would lead him to someone who could help?

After much deliberation and a despairing look toward heaven, Wesley took the path to the right. He walked along until he saw a man who was squirrel hunting. He called to him, and the hunter came over to see what was wrong. The man, it turned out, was Oscar Tatum. He and John Hooker had known one another for many years, but each of them didn't know that the other was in the area.

Wesley told Mr. Tatum that Uncle John was ill and he couldn't get him to wake up. He then told him that there was no food in the house. Oscar Tatum took Wesley to his home and fixed some sandwiches of ham and biscuits. Wesley said that they were the best biscuits that he had ever tasted!

Mr. Tatum packed up some biscuits and ham, and then went with Wesley to check on John Hooker. Upon arrival, he examined John's body and then, with compassion, explained to Wesley that his uncle had passed away — in fact, he had been dead for a few days. Wesley had thought his uncle was sleeping. While arrangements were made for John's burial, Wesley stayed with Mr. Walden and his family, who were also neighbors.

At the graveside some neighbors came together to have a Christian service to pay their respects to John Hooker. They had no knowledge of any living relative of Wesley. At the end of the service, the neighbors gathered around the freshly covered grave and discussed their dilemma: Who was going to take the boy? Someone needed to take him. Among the poor farmers living in that area of rural Missouri, "taking the boy" meant one thing — another mouth to feed. Most who lived in the rural farming communities had just enough food and clothing for their family, and nothing more.

They went from one farmer to the next, and each one said that he couldn't afford to take Wesley because he already had too many mouths to feed and provide for. Oblivious to the feelings of Wesley, each man simply stated his case. Still, they couldn't just leave him there all alone; someone had to take him. There was an unspoken code that demanded a place be found for the orphaned boy. As they came to the last man at the graveside (John Gates), he begrudgingly agreed to take the boy. There was a general sense of relief and appreciation from all the others for what they thought was Mr. Gates's generosity.

John Gates and his wife lived with their three young

children on a small farm at the edge of Risco, Missouri. The Gateses put Wesley in charge of doing most of the chores on the farm, including feeding and taking care of all the animals (milking the cows, collecting the eggs, and slopping the pigs). He was also responsible for taking care of the Gateses' young children. Wesley essentially became their slave even though he was only six years old. Work, work, work was all that Wesley knew.

Mr. and Mrs. Gates were cruel taskmasters. Wesley was not treated as a member of the family. He did not eat with the Gateses, and they did not give him appropriate clothing for the seasons. Also, they did not provide him a bed to sleep in; instead, he slept on a pallet on the floor close to the potbellied stove in order to keep warm. Wesley ate what was left over from the family's meal—when there was food left over. He would then be expected to wash the dishes, sweep the floor, and get the younger children ready for bed. At times, after the evening meal, he was sent out barefooted to help with the farm chores, even when the ground was frozen. He suffered many times from frostbite and sores on his feet. When Wesley had smallpox, Mr. Gates forced him to work out in the fields. Oftentimes Wesley was sent on errands to the store in town. Upon his arrival back home, Mrs. Gates would beat him if she thought he had taken too long to make the trip.

Wesley's father, William Frank, continued to make trips to look for his son. He asked for information about both John Hooker and Wesley everywhere he went. Though time after time, he was disappointed in his search, he never lost hope of finding his missing son.

During the time Wesley lived with the Gateses, the only positive thing in his life was that he made his first friend! Somewhere along the way, maybe at the country store or walking through the woods, he met Jim Young. Jim was about Wesley's age, and they quickly became friends. The Youngs, who had two children (Jim and a daughter), had a good-sized farm on the edge of town.

No matter how hard Wesley worked to do his chores well, it was never good enough for the Gateses. They beat him often and unmercifully. They usually took him to the barn, had him take off his shirt, and whipped him with a large strap that left his body cut and bloody. Day by day, Wesley was subjected to physical, emotional, mental, and verbal abuse. He began to wonder how much more he could endure. Never having a kind word said to him or having the personal touch of a hug was almost more than he could stand. Six years of such treatment took its toll on Wesley's body and spirit.

CHAPTER 5

RESCUED BY MR. YOUNG

The day finally came when Mrs. Gates had whipped Wesley so severely that he vowed never to let the Gateses beat him again. He had slipped away during the night and had gone to the Youngs' barn, where he had fallen into a deep sleep in the loft. The pain from Mrs. Gates's flogging had made his body raw, painful, and numb. Being physically and emotionally fatigued, Wesley was so exhausted that he didn't even hear the rooster crow early the next morning.

The Youngs' household awoke and began their morning chores. Mr. Young went out to the barn to care for the animals. Needing to give the horses and mules some hay, he climbed up into the loft. As he started to jab his pitchfork into the hay, he spotted what appeared to be part of a shoe.

Standing the pitchfork against the wall, he dug through the hay and uncovered Wesley, who was still sound asleep. Gently waking him, Mr. Young saw Wesley cringe when he sat up. Wesley explained to Mr. Young what had happened. After seeing the dried blood from the open gashes on Wesley's back, Mr. Young took him into the house. Recognizing how sore and tender Wesley was, he gently cleaned his lacerations, applied some ointment, and bandaged Wesley's wounds. Mrs. Young helped Wesley into the kitchen where she fed him a good, warm breakfast and then put him in bed.

* * *

After searching for Wesley all day, Mr. Gates came to the Youngs' home and pounded violently on the door. Wesley's eyes turned toward the door; his senses were on alert. He knew *who* was knocking. Gripped with fear, his heart was beating wildly. Would Mr. Young make him go back with Mr. Gates?

Mr. Young opened the door and stood there, blocking the way into the house. Wesley, slender in stature and malnourished, hid behind him, peeking around from time to time at Mr. Gates.

"I've come for Wesley," Mr. Gates said gruffly. "Is he here?"

"Yes, he's here." Looking over his shoulder, Mr. Young asked Wesley, "Do you want to go with Mr. Gates?"

"No, no," Wesley said, shaking his head emphatically.

Mr. Young turned again to face Mr. Gates. "You can't have Wesley. He will be staying here with our family."

"I'm taking him, so get out of my way," said Mr. Gates, trying to push Mr. Young aside.

But Mr. Young was adamant. "In order for you to take Wesley, you will have to go through me. Are you sure you want to do that?"

Mr. Gates eyed Mr. Young, straightened himself up, and clenched his fists. But seeing the determined look in the other man's eyes, he dropped his shoulders and reluctantly left.

Wesley let out a big sigh of relief. He felt safe at last!

* * *

Life with the Youngs was busy with hard work, but there was no abuse. Wesley ate every meal with the family. He was adequately clothed, and was cared for when he was sick. He worked long hours in the fields with Mr. Young and Jim, clearing "new ground," plowing with a mule, planting, chopping, and picking cotton. There was always wood to be cut for the cookstove and fireplace. There were cows to milk and other livestock to feed and water. In the evening after all the chores were done, the family would sit around and visit with one another, sharing their day's experiences, and sometimes playing checkers. Mrs. Young, sitting in her rocking chair, enjoyed watching the children play as she knitted garments for them.

* * *

In rural Missouri in the early 1900s, one-room schoolhouses were the norm where many grades studied together in a single room and were taught by a single teacher. Most states did not have mandatory attendance, and in rural areas, the school year was shorter because young people were needed to work on the farm.

During this time, the schools had few books. Instead of paper, scissors, glue sticks, markers, colored pencils, and computers, students had only chalk and a slate that they shared with other students. Discipline was usually rather strict, and learning was frequently by rote memorization. They did not have school lunch programs, but instead, students carried their lunch to school, often in a metal pail.

In the fall, Mr. Young sent Wesley, along with his own children, to school. Wesley, who had never had any schooling, wasn't sure where to go or what to do. The one-room school housed grades one through eight. Wesley, being rather tall for his age, sat with kids about his size, thinking that's where he would belong. He only knew his ABC's and numbers. When the teacher asked him to spell the name George, of course he didn't have a clue. The teacher then asked the boy behind Wesley to spell George, and the boy spelled it with ease, G-E-O-R-G-E. Then that boy leaned forward and said to Wesley, with a drawl, "Don't ya wish ya had a brother named George?"

Wesley decided that since he didn't have a brother named George, he didn't need to go to school, and the Youngs didn't insist that he go. Instead, he worked on the farm with Mr. Young. This was the only major distinction that the Youngs made between their treatment of Wesley and their own children.

*   *   *

William Frank persisted in looking for Wesley. Whenever he could, he made a trip to Arkansas or Missouri, always searching, searching for his son whom he loved so much.

*   *   *

The Youngs went to bed around seven o'clock every evening and rose early the following morning (around four thirty). Oftentimes, Mr. Young would put wood on the cookstove to get it heated for breakfast, before he headed outside to do the morning chores. Mrs. Young would make biscuits while the children were getting around.

The Industrial Revolution followed the end of the Civil War, but Mr. Young, like most farmers, still plowed and harvested with the aid of mules and draft horses. Mr. Young, Jim, and Wesley harvested their hay in June, July, and August, and stored it in the barn to feed the animals during the winter months.

Wesley's chores around the farm included helping care for the animals, working in the fields, and harvesting the crops. Mr. Young observed that Wesley was very responsible and hardworking, and that he always did more than was expected of him.

The next spring, Mr. Young gave Wesley a small plot of land in which he could plant his own crop. Wesley

Young Wesley Frank Willingham (his very first photo).

rose early and hitched the mule, ready to plow the fields. Pride swelled his heart at the responsibility given him. After his field was plowed, he planted his crop. At harvest-time, he was filled with a sense of accomplishment. He had never felt that way before. Wesley was allowed to keep the money that he made from the sale of his crop.

Mr. Young was patient with Wesley and taught him life skills. He showed

Wesley how to do basic math and how to write his name. Wesley was a quick learner. Despite having experienced years of traumatic abuse, Wesley had a kind spirit and was very cooperative. In addition to tending his own land, he continued to work with the Youngs on their farm.

Not going to school did not bother Wesley at the time—after all, he had never gone and did not know what he was missing. But one important thing was missing from his life with the Youngs. Although they were good, honest, hardworking people, the Youngs were not Christians.

CHAPTER 6

WESLEY ACCEPTS JESUS CHRIST

When Wesley was in his late teens, he saw a poster advertising a brush arbor camp revival meeting. For two weeks, all the churches in the area came together to hear an evangelist share the gospel. These meetings included a lot of music, prayer, and the message of Jesus Christ, loudly proclaimed.

Wesley had heard preaching in his early childhood days when he lived with Uncle John (who often preached and taught in the one-room schoolhouses), but since his uncle's death, there had been no personal influence of God or faith in his life. Never having been to a tent revival before, he was curious and decided to go and see what it was all about.

The large white tent was set up on a vacant lot in town. Many rows of folding chairs faced a wooden podium. Wesley found a seat among the huge crowd. The overflow of people sat on the grass along the sides of the tent. A man wearing his Sunday-best clothes stepped up to the podium. With the excitement of the evening service about to begin, the crowd hushed their chatter. The man then led the people in singing some familiar hymns. The evangelist for the revival preached about Jesus, His love for us, and His death on the cross. On a subsequent evening, the sermon was about the reality and horrors of hell.

After Wesley attended several meetings and listened to the sermons, the Holy Spirit convicted him of his sins, and he went forward and prayed to receive Jesus as his personal Savior. Even though he didn't fully understand the concept of being a Christian, he realized that he was lost and needed Jesus to save him. He went home that night and shared with the Youngs his newfound friend, Jesus Christ.

The following day while working in the field with Mr. Young, he shared again with his foster father his new faith and invited him to join him in following the Lord. Thus began a pattern of zeal in witnessing which characterized Wesley's entire life. He was baptized with many other new believers in a nearby creek. Although the water was cold, his love and fervor for the Lord were red hot, and he carried that to his last breath!

Wesley went to church as often as he could, but working the farm took most of his time. Being a farming family, the Youngs valued maximizing their time and believed going to town for church to be a waste. Wesley wanted to honor, obey, and please the Youngs; therefore, he made the decision to not go to church as often as he would have liked. Wesley loved the Youngs and was extremely thankful to God for the way they treated him as a member of their family.

* * *

One Sunday, Wesley and Jim were working in the fields. The two young men were talking back and forth while they worked. They heard the sound of a horse-drawn wagon approaching on a nearby road. Wesley glanced up and then stopped in his tracks and stared. What he saw took his breath away. *Surely, this must be a vision.* There in the wagon was the most beautiful young lady that he had ever seen! She had coal-black hair with pretty curls and a bow, a peaches-and-cream complexion, and dark brown sparkling eyes. She and her family were on their way to church.

Continuing his task, Jim called to Wesley to get back to work.

Wesley could not take his eyes off the lovely teenager. Watching the wagon until it rolled out of sight, he told Jim, "She's the prettiest girl I have ever seen, and someday I'm going to marry her."

Wesley went back to work, but his mind was on the attractive girl who had caught his attention and his heart. He had to find out who she was.

CHAPTER 7

WESLEY AND NORMA

Who was that beautiful girl in the back of the wagon? Wesley was so smitten with her that he asked around and soon learned that the family was the Phillipses who lived not too far down the road. The lovely young lady was fourteen-year-old Norma Viola Phillips (born on July 9, 1910). Norma's father was Andrew Houston Phillips, and her mother was Lula Phillips.

Wesley stayed busy on the farm, so he didn't get a chance to see Norma very often. But whenever he could he went to church, riding one of the work mules or catching a ride on a neighbor's wagon. The highlight of his week was going to church and sitting as close to Norma and her family as possible.

Norma Phillips.

Wesley was focused on one

thing and one thing only—marrying Norma. After a short period of time, Wesley asked Norma to marry him, and she accepted. Now Wesley had to get permission from her parents.

Working up every ounce of courage he could, Wesley put on a nice, clean shirt and his best coveralls, and went to ask Mr. and Mrs. Phillips for Norma's hand in marriage. As they sat in the Phillipses' living room, Wesley was literally shaking in his boots. He could feel his heart beating rapidly, as he wiped the sweat off his palms. Would Norma's parents say no? Would they think Norma was too young at fourteen years of age?

Finally Wesley stood up, looked Norma's father in the eye, and said meekly, "Mr. Phillips, I have come to ask for Norma's hand in marriage."

"No," answered Mr. Phillips, who was adamantly opposed to their marrying.

Andrew Houston and Lula Phillips.

Lula asked Houston to step into the kitchen to discuss the matter. Wesley and Norma sat quietly in anticipation. Cocking his head, Wesley strained to hear Lula and Houston's conversation. He silently prayed for their blessing and approval.

Houston thought that Norma was too young to get married. Although his wife agreed, she asserted that if they didn't give their consent, Wesley and Norma would possibly run away and get married anyway. After much deliberation and convincing, Houston finally gave his blessing.

Before Houston could change his mind, Wesley and Norma quickly went to the county courthouse to get their marriage license. They made all of the wedding preparations before the circuit preacher came to town. Rev. O. B. Miley married Wesley and Norma in the living room of the Phillipses' home on July 21, 1925.

Norma's older brother, Arlie, and his wife, Cora; her older sister, Pauline, with her husband, William; and the two younger sisters, Geneva and Verneal, attended their small ceremony. The living room was small but

Lula and Houston Phillips & the Youngs.

adequate to hold the family and a few neighbors, who witnessed the wedding. Wesley was twenty-two years old, and Norma had just turned fifteen. After the ceremony, Mrs. Phillips served some refreshments. Wesley had a sense of fulfillment. He was married to the love of his life.

*   *   *

Wesley and Norma rented a small farm with a few acres of land on the edge of Risco, Missouri. They were dependent for their livelihood on sharecropping. It was a hand-to-mouth existence, but they were happy to be together.

After working on the farm during the day, Wesley had a night job at a local grocery store, stocking the shelves after the store closed. Norma often went with him to help. She had completed the eighth grade, which was the standard education for that period of time. As Wesley worked, Norma taught him to read the labels on the cans, boxes, and other goods. She was very bright, and Wesley was eager to learn. He was an intelligent man who caught on very quickly.

One of the first books that Wesley read was the Bible. Norma helped him when he struggled with many of the words. Reading God's Word firsthand intrigued and excited Wesley. He and Norma regularly attended church; they rarely missed a service.

Lula Phillips loved Wesley as her own son. She taught him lessons from the Bible about prayer and how to draw closer to God. Her godly wisdom was Spirit taught, and she shared her knowledge with her family. She was a great spiritual mentor to Wesley.

During that first year, Lula taught Wesley how to

repair sewing machines. Wesley worked wherever he could. He took any opportunity to learn something new and to provide for himself and his young wife, whether it was farming, working at a store, or repairing other people's sewing machines. As time went by, Wesley's reading improved so much that he could read and follow instructions.

CHAPTER 8

WESLEY'S EARLY MARRIED LIFE

Wesley and Norma bought a farm just outside of Risco, Missouri, in a small community called Matthews. In addition to working the farm, Wesley — being a natural salesman — also got a job selling Rawleigh products (salves, ointments, spices, and extracts). Eleven months after Wesley and Norma were married, they welcomed their first child, a son. Howard Houston Willingham was born on June 11, 1926, in Matthews (Risco), just before Norma turned sixteen.

While they lived in Risco, Wesley and Norma had three more children: James (Jim) Andrew, born September 6, 1928, in Matthews (near Eight Ditch); Donald Eugene, born September 4, 1931; and Bonnie Sue, born January 27, 1934. Houston and Lula Phillips came and stayed with them from time to time, especially at the birth of each new baby. Wesley and Norma greatly appreciated all that her parents did to help them.

Wesley and Norma were able to buy more land, which increased the number of crops and the amount of work that was needed for the farm. Sharecroppers helped plant, care for, and harvest the crops of corn, cotton, and soybeans. Wesley and Norma also had a personal garden, as well as cows, geese, and mules.

From left, standing: Geneva Phillips, Norma & Wesley Willingham, Cora & Arlie Phillips, Pauline & Willie Cravens, and Verneal Phillips.

Seated: Houston Phillips holding Billy and Linuel Cravens and Lula Phillips holding Howard and Jim Willingham.

Having a family was very important to Wesley. He appreciated the way that the Phillips family accepted him as a son. He was also very thankful to his foster family, the Youngs, for taking him in and allowing him to be part of their family. Through the years, Wesley kept in touch with the Youngs, and his children called them "Grandpa Young" and "Grandma Young."

*   *   *

Wesley continued to sell Rawleigh products. His territory was the Matthews–Risco area. Wesley's first car was an old (used) Hudmobile with running boards on the side. Every morning, he left on his route to sell to stores and also door-to-door. Each evening, Wesley's sons would eagerly watch for their father to return home. When he turned onto the gravel road leading to the farm, the boys (Howard and Jim, along with their cousins Billy and Linuel Cravens) would run out to meet him, jump onto the running boards of the car, and ride all the way back home. What a special treat! When they arrived at the house, the boys would help unload and store the supplies to keep them safe from the weather. Wesley would then go out and help work the farm. There was always work to be done.

One time, when the boys jumped on the running board, Jim missed it and landed on the fender instead. Unable to get a good hold, he fell off the car, and Wesley ran over him. Terrified, Wesley's chest tightened as he immediately slammed on the brakes. Was Jim seriously injured? Or worse? Wesley jumped out of the car and ran to Jim's side. Kneeling down, Wesley made certain that his son was still breathing and had no broken bones. He gently placed Jim in the passenger seat and took him to the house. Bruised and very sore, Jim received special treatment for the rest of the evening. Greatly relieved, Wesley prayed a prayer of thanksgiving to God that Jim was okay.

* * *

Their farm was in the Missouri delta, and one year the Mississippi River overflowed its banks and flooded their land, ruining their crops. The following spring,

Wesley borrowed money to replant. That year there was another huge flood, and Wesley made the difficult decision to sign over the farm as payment for the debt. The family then moved to Arkansas and stayed with a distant relative of Houston's. It didn't take too long before Wesley found work.

CHAPTER 9

FINDING HIS SIBLINGS

Wesley and Norma were expecting their fifth child, and time was drawing near for the birth. A huge snowstorm blanketed the area, which made it very difficult for the doctor to get to the house, but he was in time to deliver the baby. Frankie Lou, named after both Wesley Frank and Lula Phillips, was born on January 2, 1937, in Jonesboro, Arkansas.

*   *   *

Wesley was a man of prayer. One of his daily prayers was for God to allow him to find his father's family. He had looked repeatedly but had not been able to locate them. He only had two clues: they had lived in west Texas around the turn of the century, and their family surname was Willingham.

Wesley's fervent prayer was answered in 1937. That year he was selling tobacco and other goods to stores in his territory, which included Arkansas and Texas. One day he went into a local store in Pampa, Texas.

The store clerk took one look at Wesley and said, "Your name is Willingham."

"How do you know?" asked Wesley.

"I know your brother and sisters," said the clerk. In fact, the store clerk was one of Wesley's nephews — Wesley's sister Maude's son-in-law! Wesley was the spitting image of his father, William Frank. The clerk called Wesley's brother, Lee, who immediately came to the store. Lee took Wesley to his home and contacted his sisters, Lizzie and Maude. That evening they had a huge family reunion. Wesley was finally united with his paternal family.

Wesley had found his maternal sister, Rosa Ann (Rosie), and her family in southern Missouri. He continued looking for his maternal brother, William Midget, his whole life but was unable to find him.

The year 1937 was a great year for Wesley — he found his siblings. He learned

Maude, Wesley, and Lizzie.

that his father had been a minister, and his brother and sisters — all of them Christians — had lived an ordinarily comfortable life. William Frank, who had passed away on January 2, 1922, had never stopped looking for Wesley.

*   *   *

It was very difficult to keep a job during the Great Depression, which lasted from 1929 through 1939. The tobacco company Wesley worked for went under, so he was out of work again. Having looked for work everywhere, Wesley heard that there were positions open with a petroleum company in Texas, and he drove all night to see if he could get hired. Several hundred men crowded around, applying for only twelve positions. Wesley wasn't hired, but once the other men left, Wesley talked with the manager and told him he wouldn't be able to drive back home until the following morning. He asked if he could work for no pay just to have something to do. The manager obliged, and because Wesley did such a great job and had such integrity, they hired him! The manager was impressed that Wesley was willing to work without pay just to keep himself busy. Having found work, Wesley moved his family to Texas.

*   *   *

After working at the petroleum company for several months, Wesley contacted the Singer Manufacturing Company for information on where the best place would be to open a store. After much discussion, they decided that Kennett, Missouri, was a good location. Therefore, the family moved to Kennett. Wesley owned his own Singer sewing machine store, where he sold, repaired, and serviced sewing machines. Wesley had so much wisdom and common sense. His outgoing, persuasive personality made him a natural salesman. Wesley was honest and hardworking, and because he always told the truth, he gained the trust and business of his customers. They respected him, and his number of clients grew.

The Pearcy family (Norma's sister Geneva, her husband, Richard, and their four daughters, Reta, Sherma Jean, Martha Lou, and Patricia) also moved to Kennett. Richard helped Wesley at the sewing machine store. The two families lived close to one another and were always there for each other. They essentially were one big family.

Norma owned and operated her own lunch counter right next door to the Singer sewing machine store. The area where customers ate their lunch was quite narrow with limited space for tables and chairs. The long counter had stools for the customers to sit on. The menu was mostly soups and sandwiches. Wesley would come over just before the lunch crowd to get his lunch.

Norma took her youngest daughter, Frankie, to the restaurant with her every day. The other children were all in school. Frankie loved being there when the vendors

Norma (in front) is seated at the counter with Frankie beside her. Wesley is standing on the right.

came in bringing candy, chips, nuts, and other items for sale because sometimes they would give her samples. When the noon crowd came, Norma would fix Frankie's lunch and have her sit on the back steps (to keep her out of the way). If Wesley didn't have any customers of his own, he would walk next door to the lunch counter. He thoroughly enjoyed visiting with the noon crowd, and often gained their sewing machine business.

Wesley also owned a gas station and a larger restaurant in the town square beside the Ely and Walker Shirt Factory. The factory employees packed the restaurant every day for lunch. Early each morning, the older children helped Norma prepare the sandwiches and other food. The older kids helped to wait tables in the summertime. Whenever needed, Wesley and Norma hired help. In the evenings, Norma and the children, along with the Pearcy girls, made cotton sacks, which Wesley sold to the farmers.

After the bombing of Pearl Harbor in December 1941, the United States joined World War II. Because of the war effort, the Singer Sewing Machine Company changed its focus to weapons manufacturing for the military. As a result, Wesley could no longer receive new sewing machines or get parts for the repairs. Therefore, he had to close the store.

CHAPTER 10

NORMA BECOMES SERIOUSLY ILL

Wesley got a job with the J. R. Watkins Company selling their products (lotions, liniments, cosmetics, and spices) door-to-door in order to provide for his growing family.

He did a lot of traveling and wasn't home much, except on weekends. He loved being around people and being able to help them.

Wesley worked very hard, and the Watkins Company recognized his work ethic, so it wasn't long before they promoted him to regional supervisor. His region, which included southern Missouri and northeastern Oklahoma, involved

Back row (from left): Jim, Howard.
Front row: Donald, Frankie, Bonnie.

traveling long distances. Wesley's desire was to be home every weekend, but sometimes he traveled so far that he was not able to return home for two weeks at a time.

* * *

While living in Kennett, Missouri, Norma had two miscarriages. The second one was very difficult for her, and she almost hemorrhaged to death. Not long afterward, she became pregnant again with her last baby, Phillip Lee, who was born on January 5, 1943. Because of Norma's poor health, Geneva and her family moved in with the Willinghams to make it easier for her to take care of both families.

After Phillip's birth, Norma wasn't able to regain her health, so Wesley took her to the country doctor who had delivered Phillip. Thinking she was just lazy, the doctor told her to go home and get busy. What the doctor didn't know was that Norma was one of the hardest-working women anywhere and she didn't have a lazy bone in her body. Norma went home and tried to take care of her family and household responsibilities, but she just wasn't able to be up on her feet for any amount of time. Therefore, accomplishing any household chore was impossible for her. Not being able to care for her family, Norma became depressed.

Wesley and Norma.

Living nearby in Cape Girardeau, Missouri, both

Lula Phillips (Norma's mother) and Pauline Cravens (Norma's sister) came to see what they could do to help. They took one look at Norma and decided to take her to Cape Girardeau for a second opinion. They arrived at Lula's home, and the next morning they took Norma to the doctor. The doctor took one look at her and said, "I know exactly what is wrong. She has contracted tuberculosis." An x-ray revealed that Norma only had half of one lung remaining.

In early March, the doctor made arrangements for Wesley to take Norma to the sanatorium in Mt. Vernon, Missouri. This was devastating news for the whole family, and Wesley was beside himself. The thought of admitting his beloved wife to a sanatorium was more than he could fathom. Also, was the question: How was he going to care for his children? The family was too large for Geneva to take care of the six Willingham children along with her own four daughters for any length of time.

CHAPTER 11

SAYING GOODBYE

Once the school year was finished, the family had a meeting and suggested that Wesley divide the children up to live with different relatives. This wasn't Wesley's desire, but his job as a traveling manager for the Watkins Company kept him away from home for a week at a time. Even as he began the grieving process for his beloved wife's failing health, he felt he had no choice but to go along with the proposal.

Wesley's heart was broken when he realized that his children would have to be divided among different family members. Howard, along with Philip Lee (the baby), went to live with Pauline and William Cravens in Cape Girardeau. Norma, knowing she was dying, had given baby Phillip Lee to her eldest sister, Pauline, for her to raise as her own. She knew that Wesley's job kept him away from home and he would not be able to care for their infant son. Jim went to live with Geneva and Richard Pearce, who had moved to Bonham, Texas. Grandmother Phillips decided to keep the "three babies," as she always referred to Donald, Bonnie, and Frankie. Lula told Houston that, as soon as possible, she wanted to live in Mt. Vernon to be close to Norma. He agreed, and they found a small apartment over a store in the town square not far from the hospital. Wesley was thankful to God that his children had loving families to live with.

Lula and Houston moved with the "three babies" into the scantily furnished apartment that was small and dark, but adequate. The one single light that hung from the living room made it difficult to see in the evenings. There was an unfinished loft, where Bonnie and Frankie played with paper dolls they cut from the Sears & Roebuck catalog. Lula took Donald, Bonnie, and Frankie to school to get them enrolled. Houston would walk the girls to school in the mornings.

*   *   *

The sanatorium was in a beautiful setting on a hill. Norma's room was in the cold, damp basement. Every day Lula fixed a good hot lunch for Norma and her roommate — both were terminally ill. She walked several blocks to the hospital, climbed the many steps, turned to the right, and followed the sidewalk around to the building where her daughter's room was. She tried to keep the tone light, and would often joke with Norma and her roommate to keep their spirits up. When Donald, Bonnie, and Frankie went to the hospital to visit their mother, they had to see and talk with her through a small screened window that was close to the ground.

Wesley came to see Norma and the children every weekend possible. Since he couldn't do anything to help his wife, he did the only thing he could do: continue to work and provide for his family. He kept as close contact as he could with each family. As he rode the roller coaster of grief and experienced many different emotions, he continued to ask God the question *why*. He was lost, torn, and overwhelmed with many broken dreams. While Norma lived out her final days in the sanatorium, Wesley was having to face the eventual death of his wife, the end of their family life as they had known it, and the uncertainty of what lay ahead for him and his six children.

*   *   *

Pauline and William Cravens were going through a difficult time. Linuel, their second son, had contracted spinal meningitis. Hospitalized in Cape Girardeau, he was near death. Someone from the family was at the hospital at all times. Because of this dire situation, they asked Verneal (Pauline and Norma's youngest sister, who lived in Sikeston, Missouri) if she could temporarily take care of Baby Philip Lee. Linuel was so ill they weren't sure if the Lord was going to take him home or heal him. It was very stressful for everyone. Eventually Linuel's health improved slightly, but he was still in critical condition. It was several weeks before he improved enough for him to return home. By that time, Verneal and Howard McGill had become so attached to Phillip Lee that Pauline and William reluctantly decided to allow him to stay with them.

*   *   *

Norma's health slowly declined every day. Though it was difficult to watch her go through all she was suffering, it became evident that she was ready to go to her heavenly home. On November 3, 1943, she passed away into the arms of Jesus. Lula was very distraught, but she drew on the Lord's strength. She composed herself enough to call a taxi so she could go to the school to pick up Donald, Bonnie, and Frankie. Houston went to the apartment to get everything ready for their move back to Cape Girardeau.

Norma's funeral was held in Sikeston, Missouri, with the whole family coming together to grieve her passing. Afterward, Lula and Houston returned with Donald, Bonnie, and Frankie to their home in Cape Girardeau. Howard went back to Pauline and William Cravens's home, and Jim returned to the Pearces' home.

Verneal and Howard wanted to adopt Phillip Lee because he had now been in their home for about six months and they had become very close to him. Shortly after Norma's passing, they had the adoption papers drawn up, which they then presented to Wesley. He was extremely hesitant, but not knowing what the future held or how he was going to get his children all together again, he reluctantly signed the papers. This was one decision Wesley regretted his whole life.

Norma's last breath inevitably changed the family. No longer having your mother can be paralyzing, and Norma left behind a husband and six children whose ages ranged from eleven months to seventeen years old. Being without her caused everyone to take life more seriously. It does not matter how self-confident you are—losing a mother deprives you of a chief cheerleader. Norma was the glue that held the family together. Wesley and the whole family felt her loss in a deeply profound way. Lula and Houston were devastated with the loss of their daughter, but they carried on for the children.

Wesley returned to his supervisor position with Watkins. He wasn't afforded much time to grieve the death of his wife. This was a difficult time for the whole family, and being separated didn't help either. Wesley loved and missed his wife and children. He continued to try to find a way to bring the family together again.

CHAPTER 12

WESLEY'S BLENDED FAMILY

Wesley sent money to each family on a regular basis to help with the expenses of raising his children. While working in Oklahoma with one of his Watkins Associates (James Melton Colvin), Wesley met James's daughter Vera Dean Colvin Gibson (born October 28, 1923). She was only twenty years old and the youngest in a family of fourteen children. She had two small children from a previous marriage: Irvin Junior (Junior was his middle name) who was four years old and Rowina Lee (Sissy) who was two years old. Wesley was very infatuated with Vera Dean (Deanie), and he loved being with her and her children.

It wasn't long before Wesley and Deanie realized they wanted to spend their life together, so in early 1944, they joined their families. Wesley accepted Deanie's children and took them as his own. Now he eagerly began bringing his family back together again. Howard and Jim, along with Junior and Sissy, joined Wesley and Deanie in their apartment in Ada, Oklahoma. Since

Howard and Jim were only a few years younger than Deanie, Wesley told them that they didn't have to call her "Mom" but they had to respect and help her around the house when she asked. Deanie became pregnant in February, and Wesley looked forward to having another child for him to love.

In March of 1944, Wesley, Deanie, and the family moved from the apartment into a large two-story house with a spacious basement and nice yard. This allowed Wesley to go to Cape Girardeau to bring Donald, Bonnie, and Frankie to their new home. (Grandma Phillips was very sad that she would no longer have her "babies" to care for.) Now, they were one large blended family. A part of Wesley missed and would always love Norma; but, once again, peace and contentment shone on his face. His family was all together again.

Wesley and Deanie with his foster parents, the Youngs.

That spring, the family had a big Easter egg hunt. Early Sunday morning Howard and Jim went outside and hid the eggs in the front yard. Once all the eggs were hidden, the other children were allowed to come out and begin the hunt. Wesley, Jim, and Howard helped the three younger children as they hunted for the eggs. Howard took Frankie on his shoulders, and Jim helped Junior as he searched in the bushes. The whole family laughed a lot and enjoyed this special time together. Wesley was the biggest kid of all and enjoyed helping Sissy find her eggs. After all the eggs were found, they went inside and ate breakfast, which Deanie had prepared. Then, dressed up in their new Easter outfits, the family went to church and celebrated Jesus's resurrection. When they returned home, they ate a hearty dinner, which included the Easter eggs.

*   *   *

Donald was at an in-between age, not quite old enough to fit in with Howard and Jim, and too old to play with his younger siblings. Not wanting Donald to feel alone and left out, Wesley brought a little brown and white puppy home for him to care for. Donald loved his new friend and spent many hours playing and caring for it. The puppy followed Donald around; they were inseparable. When Donald wasn't home, the puppy stayed in the basement.

Deanie's regular routine, every Monday morning, was to do the laundry in the basement. She separated the clothes to be washed into piles according to colors. Unbeknownst to anyone, the puppy climbed into one of the piles, and Deanie put those clothes into the washer. (They had an electric wringer washing machine. The machine had a wringer attached to the round tub. After the clothes were washed, they would be put through the wringer into the rinse water. This was done three times to get as much of the water out as possible. Then the clothes would be hung outside on a line to dry.) It wasn't until Deanie was putting the clothes through the wringer that she discovered the dead puppy. She felt terrible, and Donald was devastated.

When Wesley came home that weekend, he comforted Donald with sympathy and compassion. Donald got a lot of one-on-one time with his Dad that weekend, which really helped with his grief over the loss of his puppy.

* * *

World War II escalated during Howard's senior year in high school, and he wanted to drop out of school and join the United States Navy. Wesley wanted Howard to stay and finish his education first, but Howard's patriotic fervor compelled him to help our country in the war effort. Hearing his son's passionate explanation, Wesley gave his blessing for him to enlist.

* * *

Late one afternoon, while Frankie was doing her home-work in the upstairs bedroom, Junior came in to pester her — as he often did — and sat over by the screened window.

"Junior, you shouldn't lean on the screen. You might fall out," Frankie remarked.

The words had just come out of her mouth, when Junior gave the screen a big push, and sure enough, he fell out of the window, rolled down the roof, hit the edge of the steps, and lay unconscious on the sidewalk.

Deanie wasn't at home; she was at a maternity doctor's appointment. Bonnie was the oldest child at home at the time.

Frankie ran down the stairs, screaming, "Junior fell out the window!"

As she and Bonnie ran outside, they found Junior lying lifeless on the sidewalk. Bonnie picked him up, carried him inside, and laid him on the couch. She immediately called the doctor's office and summoned Deanie home.

Finding Junior still unconscious when she arrived home, Deanie called the doctor, who came as quickly as he could to the house. After examining Junior, the doctor said there was nothing more he could do except pray.

Wesley was out of town on one of his routes when he received a strong impression from God that he should call home. In those days, there were very few telephones available. That night, when he returned to the hotel, he called home and found out what had happened. Without hesitation, Wesley threw his clothes in the suitcase, jumped in his car, and headed home. He drove several hours before stopping for the night.

Rising early the next morning, he continued his journey. Several church members had come to the house and prayed over Junior, who still lay unconscious. The doctor returned every evening to check on him.

When Wesley got home, he immediately went over to the couch where Junior was lying, and prayed aloud over him. Immediately after Wesley said, "Amen," Junior slowly opened his eyes and regained consciousness. Praise God, Junior was okay! In later years, Junior (also known as Jay) had his last name legally changed to Willingham.

* * *

In the summer of 1944, Wesley moved the family to Sasakwa, Oklahoma, to a farm on the edge of town. They had pigs, chickens, cows, a mule, a horse, and a large garden. There was also a nice apple orchard. Wesley helped Jim and Donald with the farm work whenever he was home. Early Saturday mornings, Jim and Donald would get up early and go hunting for squirrels and rabbits. Good eating!

During the first week of November 1944, the birth of the baby was drawing close. Wesley, still traveling with the Watkins Company, was uneasy about leaving the house. Deanie had had a difficult pregnancy and had been bedridden for the last two months. Before Wesley drove away, he promised to call as often as he could to check on her.

Thankfully on Friday, November 10, 1944, a healthy baby girl was born at the hospital in Ada, Oklahoma. Wesley and Deanie had not yet decided on a name for the new baby, so with Wesley being gone, Deanie asked Jim what he wanted to name her. Jim happened to be dating a girl named Mary Linda, and he liked that name, so the baby was named Mary Linda. Wesley arrived home the next day and went directly to the hospital to see his wife and new daughter.

CHAPTER 13

WESLEY SURRENDERS TO PREACH

Wesley surrendered to preach the gospel in 1944 while living in Sasakwa. He had been feeling the call to ministry for several years, but admitted that he had been running from it because he felt that he wasn't qualified. Being self-educated, Wesley believed he didn't know enough about the Bible. Nevertheless, he responded to God's calling and was ordained by the Free Will Baptist denomination. Although Wesley continued working for Watkins, he began preaching whenever the opportunity arose. He told everyone he met about Jesus.

Wesley believed the Bible was God's instruction book for his life. He always did his best to follow the commandments and directives provided in God's Word. He took his role and responsibility as a father very seriously. As a parent, Wesley was a strong disciplinarian. He wanted his children to be respectful to adults. When correcting his children, he gave them three warnings. The first directive was "Stop doing that." The second was "I told you to stop that, and if I have to speak to you again, you will get a spanking." All his children knew that he always followed through on what he said. The third time, Wesley would take the disobedient child into the bathroom, where he applied the "board of education." Wesley would say, "This hurts me more than it hurts you." After the memorable spanking was administered, Wesley told the child how much he loved him. Wesley believed disciplining children was supported in the Bible—God disciplines His children because He loves them, and God directs parents to likewise discipline their children. Therefore, he spanked his children out of obedience to God and because he loved them. He knew the difference between discipline and abuse. Even though Wesley had been terribly abused as a child, with God's help he did not abuse his own children.

* * *

One weekend, one of the new believers at the church came by their home. The man was a heavy smoker, and Wesley shared with him that a Christian's body is the temple of the Holy Spirit. Wesley told the man, "I think that you should give up smoking because smoking is harmful to your body."

"Well, *you* drink coffee, and that can't be good for you," the man replied.

"If this offends you, and you think that I should give up coffee, I will."

"Yes, I do."

"Okay, I'll give up coffee," said Wesley. And he did. He didn't drink coffee again until he and his family moved out of the area.

* * *

After graduating from high school in Sasakwa, Wesley's second eldest son, Jim, was offered a contract to play with the Chicago Cubs Major League Baseball team, starting out in their minor league in Texas. Jim went to his father for input and advice. Wesley told him that it was his decision to make. He advised Jim to seek God's guidance and be sure this was God's will for his life. Jim took the bus to Texas, visited with the team, and talked with the manager. Ultimately, he decided to join the United States Marine Corps instead. After serving in the military, Jim went to the University of Missouri on a sports scholarship and the G.I. Bill.

* * *

Wesley's Ordination Certificate, February 24, 1946.

During the summer of 1945, a small Free Will Baptist church in Earlsboro, Oklahoma, called Wesley to be their pastor. This was Wesley's first pastorate. Wanting to do God's bidding, he was both excited and nervous. Wesley moved his family, and they lived in the parsonage next door to the church for three months. The biggest industry in the area was drilling and pumping for oil, so there were oil rigs all around Earlsboro. The pumping sound of the oil wells put the children to sleep at night.

Wesley worked a full-time job as well as pastoring the church. Bi-vocational pastors were very common in the 1940s and 1950s for small churches. With Wesley being gone during most of the week, many of the pastoral duties were left to Deanie, and she rose to the task. She took food to the sick and visited the newcomers who came to the church.

After selling Watkins' products during the day, Wesley would prepare his messages in his hotel room in the evenings. He depended completely on God to know what to preach on Sunday mornings. He would do his best to be home on Wednesday nights, but at times, it was difficult. But he was always home on the weekends to preach every Sunday morning and Sunday night. Under Wesley's leadership, the little church grew, and the people loved Wesley and his family.

Watkins managers awards dinner. Wesley is second from the right on the second row.

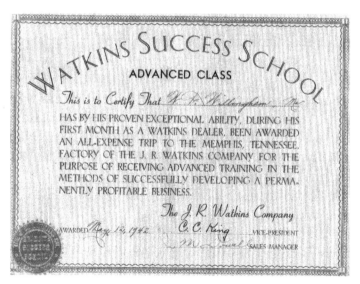

Watkins certificate, May 12, 1942.

CHAPTER 14

SPIRITUAL GROWTH

After three months in Earlsboro, the Watkins Company moved Wesley's territory to the Mountain Grove, Missouri, area. Their home in Mountain Grove had three bedrooms and a big potbellied stove in the living room. Not uncommon for the area, an outhouse was used as their bathroom, and the pages from the Sears & Roebuck catalog were used as toilet paper. There was a water pump at the kitchen sink. On the wall opposite to where Frankie and Bonnie sat at the dinner table, Bonnie taped a sign that said "Be sure to heat water in the teakettle." This was a reminder to heat the water while they were eating so it would be hot when they were ready to wash the dishes.

On Saturday nights Deanie would bring in the large round tub, place it in the dining room, and fill it with hot water. Then each one of the kids would take their weekly bath in the same water. After living there for a year, Wesley had a bathroom built with a toilet, a tub, and a hot water heater! With the bathroom complete, each child could take a bath in clean water. Wesley also had a faucet installed at the kitchen sink, which made hot and cold water available. This made the girls ecstatic — hot water in the kitchen made doing the dishes much easier.

* * *

After being honorably discharged from the navy, Wesley's son, Howard, moved to Flat River, Missouri, where he met and fell in love with Peggy Kennon. He went to Mr. Kennon and asked his permission for Peggy's hand in marriage — which he gave — and Peggy excitedly accepted. Wanting his father to perform the ceremony, Howard and Peggy traveled to Mountain Grove for a few days. Wesley planned to return home for the wedding, but circumstances with Watkins made it impossible for him to arrive in time. This upset and disappointed Wesley. It would have been his first time conducting a wedding, and he had looked forward to the special honor of marrying his son and future daughter-in-law. Deanie quickly made arrangements for a local pastor friend to come and perform the ceremony. She prepared a cake and refreshments for a small reception afterward.

* * *

Wesley was a guest preacher from time to time at different churches. On Sunday mornings, he also did a radio broadcast from the living room where he preached the good news about Jesus. The Franklin family came to the house and sang for the broadcast, and then Wesley delivered the sermon. After the broadcast, Wesley and his family attended the regular Sunday service at the local church.

* * *

In 1948, while the family was living in Mountain Grove, Missouri, a small country church (Dry Creek, out from Willow Springs, Missouri) called Wesley to be their pastor. This led the family to move to Willow Springs.

By this time, Donald had moved to Springfield, Missouri, where he attended Drury College for a year. Afterward, he joined the United States Navy.

One Sunday afternoon the church at Dry Creek had a baptismal service at the river. After the crowd gathered, they sang the hymn "Shall We Gather at the River," and Wesley gave a sermonette and then baptized twelve people, including three of his daughters — Frankie Lou, Sissy (Rowina Lee), and Mary Linda.

While the family lived in Willow Springs, there were

Wesley is baptizing Mary Linda. Next in line is Sissy and then Frankie.

times when hobos would stop by the house, wanting food. Wesley always welcomed the men, but he would have them help him with odd jobs while Deanie fixed their lunch. Wesley never sent the hobos off without sharing the gospel and giving them some extra food for the road.

Wesley had a portable Underwood typewriter, and he learned to type very fast using his two index fingers. One time he needed to create a two-page contract, so he just typed it up. Afterward, the contract looked as if a professional attorney had drawn it up! Wesley took some Bible correspondence courses and always typed his homework. He made good grades in the courses, which was amazing since he didn't have any formal education. However, he spelled phonetically, so oftentimes his words were misspelled. He also used that little typewriter to type his sermon notes.

* * *

When quarterly grades were recorded at the local school, all the children brought home their report cards. School-work was a breeze for Bonnie and Junior. They enjoyed learning, and their grades were always straight As.

Frankie earned average grades because she experienced difficulties in learning. Years later, she was diagnosed as being dyslexic.

Trying to encourage Frankie to do better, Deanie said, "Why can't you get grades like them (meaning Bonnie and Junior)? What is the matter with you?"

Frankie's spirit was crushed, and she ran outside in tears with her report card.

Wesley was outside working on a project and saw her crying. He hugged her and asked, "What's wrong, Sweetheart?"

"My report card isn't very good."

"Did you do the best you could?" said Wesley, as he looked at Frankie's card.

"Yes."

Looking at Frankie with compassion and love, Wesley told her, "I am proud of Bonnie and Junior for their good grades. You might not be as book smart as they are, but you have more common sense than both of them put together. And you can figure things out a lot of times when they can't."

Wesley had such empathy and godly wisdom. He was able to comfort Frankie and make her feel so much better. He told her, "Always do your best. Everything else will be alright." Wesley had such a way of making people feel heard and understood. He listened not only with his ears but also with his heart. It was that humility and compassionate spirit that often drew people to him.

* * *

It was difficult for Wesley to find a space for his daily morning quiet time with God, so he chose the downstairs bathroom. Every morning, without fail, he prayed aloud for his family. He had such a close walk with his Heavenly Father, and that relationship made him passionate about his role of husband and father. Wesley was very fervent and enthusiastic as he prayed for his wife, children, and other people. Frankie remembers waking up, hearing her father praying, and waiting for her name to be called. What a wonderful peace that brought Wesley's family to hear him pray aloud for each one of them.

CHAPTER 15

FINDING JOHN GATES

Wesley came home every weekend to preach at the Dry Creek church. The time eventually came when Watkins wanted him to have a larger territory where he wouldn't be able to go home every weekend. His manager informed Wesley that he either had to quit their company or quit pastoring the church. Wesley told them that he would not quit pastoring, so they let him go.

This was a huge disappointment. Wesley was upset and a little angry. He realized though that being faithful to what God had called him to do was more important than allowing any company to pressure him into disobeying God. He had faith, knowing God promised that if he would stay true to Him during this time of uncertainty, God would provide. The church really came together and brought all kinds of fruits, vegetables, and meat for the family. God continued to supply all their needs.

Being let go from Watkins brought on feelings of bitterness and resentment in Wesley, which were foreign to his nature. Hurt, puzzled, and distressed, he decided he was going to find John Gates and confront him. He wanted to show him that he had turned out well, even though Mr. Gates had been extremely abusive to him. He located John Gates in southeastern Missouri and went to his house. When Wesley arrived, he was surprised at what he saw. An elderly, feeble, mostly blind man sat on the front porch.

Walking up the steps, Wesley called out, "Hello."

Recognizing Wesley's voice, Mr. Gates said, "Wesley, is that you? Please, don't hurt me."

All of Wesley's anger and resentment dissolved in pity toward this wretched man. In that moment, God gave Wesley such peace, which enabled him in turn to show grace and mercy to Mr. Gates. Wesley offered him love and forgiveness, and told him about God's love for him. They sat on the porch, talking for about an hour. Before Wesley left, John Gates prayed to receive Jesus as his personal Savior.

Thanking God for allowing him the opportunity to share about His Son, Wesley returned home, feeling closer to God. This encounter allowed him to close that chapter of his life, with God being honored and glorified in the end.

CHAPTER 16

ALWAYS DOING GOD'S BUSINESS

The General Baptist Association asked Wesley to plant a church in Willow Springs. He went around and talked to the neighbors about starting a new church, presenting the gospel to all who would listen. In the beginning, the church met in Wesley's home. The General Baptist Association bought property for the church site. While pastoring this church, Wesley almost single-handedly built the church building. He took seminary courses through the mail to further his Biblical education and to help him in the ministry.

As a church-planting minister, Wesley received a small salary from the General Baptist Association. He also had a business of repairing and selling sewing machines in order to bring in additional income to support his family.

After graduating from high school in Willow Springs, Missouri, Bonnie received a scholarship and moved to Cape Girardeau, where she went to Southeast Missouri State University. Living with her grandmother, Lula

Phillips (Houston had passed away), Bonnie graduated in three years, while working full-time to pay for her degree in teaching.

The family's time in Willow Springs came to an end when Collins Chapel General Baptist Church in Poplar Bluff, Missouri, called Wesley to be their pastor. Relocating the rest of the family to Poplar Bluff, Wesley began the full-time pastorate. He worked daily at the church, ministering to the sick, acting as church custodian, preparing messages, visiting his flock, and performing wedding ceremonies. He was always the first at the church in the morning and the last one to leave. The congregation grew under Wesley's leadership.

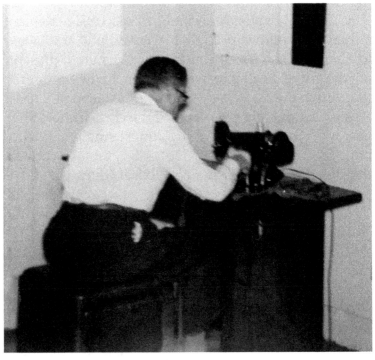

Wesley repairing a sewing machine.

After two-and-a-half years, the First General Baptist Church in Poplar Bluff called Wesley to be their pastor. The family lived in Poplar Bluff for a total of four years (1951 to 1955).

After graduating from high school, Frankie moved to Saint Louis, Missouri, for employment opportunities.

In the summer of 1955, the family moved to Flat River, Missouri. Wesley felt God leading him to open a furniture and sewing machine store. He enjoyed working on sewing machines, but he mostly enjoyed the interaction with his customers. Sensitive to God's leading, he shared the gospel of Jesus Christ with most customers.

In the spring of 1957, the General Baptist church in Santa Ana, California, called Wesley to be their pastor. Wesley accepted the call, and the family moved into the parsonage. The children still remaining at home were Jay (Junior), Sissy (Rowina Lee), and Mary Linda.

CHAPTER 17

DRAWING CLOSER TO GOD

Wesley bought a home in Santa Ana, California, where he started a new church plant in 1959. In 1967 Wesley and Deanie moved to Willow Springs, Missouri, to pastor the church he had founded in 1949.

Wesley and Deanie.

Wesley finally semiretired from pastoral duties in 1973. Howard's wife, Peggy, became ill with cancer and needed help with the children, so Wesley and Deanie bought a home and moved back to Santa Ana. During the remaining years of his life, Wesley continued pastoring and interim-pastoring different churches.

He opened a sewing machine and vacuum repair shop in Costa Mesa, California, in 1973. He named the store Sincere Sewing Machine. He chose that name because he knew it would appear before Singer Sewing Machine in the phone book. He had great wisdom and a good dose of business sense too! He always told customers about Jesus, and they knew that they could expect honesty and great service from Wesley.

After giving the Sincere Sewing Machine store to Howard, Wesley worked from his garage repairing sewing machines and vacuum cleaners. He was successful in every aspect of his life, not so much financially, but in the lives he invested in. But business was never his first love—God, family, and people were. Anyone who knew him, even slightly, knew *that*. Wesley was always accommodating, and he would do anything for his family.

*   *   *

Jim owned a car dealership (Long Beach Boulevard Buick) in Long Beach, California, and he gave Wesley and Deanie a new car every couple of years. Every time the car needed service or every time Wesley had a chance, he would visit Jim at the car dealership. Sometimes, Jim would be in a meeting and would not be able to get away. While Wesley was waiting, he would share the gospel with Jim's employees—with any that would listen.

Jim told his father, "You can't do that, Daddy."

"Why not?" Wesley replied.

Jim explained to his father that (1) his employees were supposed to be working, and (2) he had employees from various religious backgrounds and it made some of them uncomfortable. However, whenever the opportunity arose in his conversations with Jim's employees, Wesley continued to share about Jesus.

*   *   *

Jim and Wesley playing checkers.

In the 1970s, Wesley drove to Missouri to speak in a revival meeting. On the way, he stopped in Texas to visit with his daughter Mary Linda and her husband, Lynn. Wesley told Lynn that there was a family living in the area who had purchased a sewing machine from him in California. After the family had moved to Texas, they had stopped making their payments. Wesley wanted to visit the couple and collect the money. It had been two years since the family had purchased the sewing machine, so Lynn thought there was no way to recoup the loss. But out of respect for his father-in-law, Lynn drove him to the couple's home. When they arrived at the house, Lynn stayed in the car and watched as Wesley went up to the door. After talking with the couple for a little while, Wesley came away with a check for the full amount owed him. Lynn was flabbergasted.

* * *

Wesley had a wonderful, outgoing personality; he was engaging, warm, and compassionate. He never met a stranger. When Wesley met someone, he would introduce himself as "Old Man Preacher Willingham." He made people feel so comfortable that they would share about their life with him. After talking with someone for a few minutes, Wesley would say, "I have a good friend I would like to introduce you to." Wesley would proceed to tell about the most important person in his life—Jesus Christ. It always made his heart so happy when he shared with someone about Jesus and that person accepted God's invitation of salvation.

Throughout his life, Wesley had a desire to see souls saved. As he stated in a sermon, he was concerned that the world was "standing in dire need today for the old-time, Holy Ghost, God-sent salvation—people that will preach the word of God and are not ashamed of it. I have nothing to be ashamed of. I have no apologies. [You say] 'Well, Brother Willingham, you ought to apologize to all of us and not preach anymore like you did.' I say, 'Sassafras!' on that. The only person I owe is God. I'm free as a bird, praise the Lord! Saved and on my way to heaven, and glad of it."

Wesley was a joy-filled Christian. He unashamedly and unapologetically lived for Christ. His everyday conversations were filled with references to the goodness of the Lord. One of his trademarks was singing or whistling the hymns of the faith: "Amazing Grace," "Oh, How I Love Jesus," "When the Roll Is Called Up Yonder," and

"Victory in Jesus." He knew all the verses by memory. His faith did not alter with circumstances. He sang when changing flat tires in the rain. He sang in the face of death when he was left with six motherless children. Easter was not just a sentimental story to Wesley; Easter was a reality. He lived out his faith every day of his life.

Two very special men—his brothers-in-law Richard Pearcy and William Cravens—influenced his life greatly. They were not only family members but also close friends. All three of these men answered God's call to the ministry; therefore, they had a special bond.

Wesley told several people over the course of his life that the one thing he was remorseful of was signing the adoption papers so that Verneal and Howard could adopt Phillip Lee. Although he knew that he needed family assistance with the children when Norma became ill, he never wanted to give any of his children to anyone. In Wesley's mind, separating his children was just supposed to be a temporary situation. Wesley carried a picture of Philip Lee in his wallet until the time of his death.

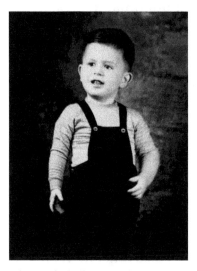

Photo of Phillip Lee that Wesley carried in his wallet.

The church at Dry Creek, Wesley's second pastorate.

First General Baptist Church in Willow Springs. This is the building that Wesley almost single-handedly built.

Collins Chapel General Baptist Church in Poplar Bluff, Missouri.

Back row: Wesley, Deanie, and Frankie.

Front row: Sissy, Mary Linda, and Junior.

Wesley's Children and Their Spouses

From left: Howard, Jean, Cecil, Frankie, Jim, Sissy, Bonnie, Jim, Betty, Jim, Jay, Sharon, Don, and Helen.

Seated: Charles & Deanie Chatoney, and Mary Linda.

Back row, from left: Sissy, Frankie, and Bonnie.
Front row: Mary Linda, Jay, Jim, Donald, and Howard.

From left: Mary Linda, Bonnie, Sissy, Jim, Frankie, Phillip Lee, and Jay at Don and Helen's funeral service.

CHAPTER 18

WESLEY'S HOMEGOING

While living in Santa Ana, California, Wesley suffered a massive stroke, and on September 1, 1980, at the age of seventy-eight, God called him to his heavenly home. His nine children, their spouses, his twenty-nine grandchildren, and a host of other family and friends gathered together for a celebration of his life. So many people came to the service at the funeral home chapel that there was not enough room for everyone to come inside. Wesley was so beloved and respected that many people who came to the funeral were not able to come in and instead stood outside the chapel. After the service, people made their way to the front to view the body and to give their condolences to Deanie. Half an hour later, the funeral director came and said, "We're very sorry, but we are going to have to cut this off. Another funeral was supposed to have started thirty minutes ago."

Gathering around the freshly dug grave, the family and close friends paid a final tribute, honoring "The Preacher," whose life was a sermon. A neighbor's eulogy was read, a part of which follows: "The Preacher was an elderly man who stood tall and erect, and always appeared to have his whole world in total control. . . . The Preacher was a man who, just by walking amongst us, seemed to radiate God's light."

Wesley left little money, being a generous man who gave to those in need. However, he did leave a legacy — a legacy of love for God, love for music, and love for others. He lived a selfless life, well lived and worth emulating — full of integrity! He was a godly man.

> Blessed is a man who perseveres under trial; for once he has been approved, he will receive the crown of life which the Lord has promised to those who love Him. (James 1:12 NASB)

The following poem was written by Wesley's granddaughter Carol Wyatt (McGown) on September 1, 1980:

To Gram & Grandpa, I love you.

Time For Joy

Time for joy, time for cheer,
That is why we all are here.

We've known this loved one, and we've known his love,
And we'll all make it through this with help from above.

We should rejoice, we should not grieve,
For it is God's will that he should leave.

Although we want him for our own,
He'll be so much happier in his new home.

We cannot ask for him to stay.
Let's not be selfish. Let him go away.

We've had him here on earth for many wonderful years.
Let him see us smiling, not shedding our tears.

We must let go now, we can't hold on.
We'll see him again soon. I know it won't be long.

Time for joy, time for cheer,
That is why we all are here.

We've known this loved one, and we've known his love,
And we'll all make it through this with help from above.

Thanks for everything,
Carol

Wesley Frank Willingham.
August 12, 1902–September 1, 1980.

This letter was written by Wesley's neighbor Pat Slocum:

The Preacher

We live in a quiet, uneventful neighborhood on the edge of Santa Ana. Unlike most of southern California, ours is a neighborhood that consists of many friendships and people who care about each other.

This week was more eventful than most, as early Saturday a.m., we were awakened by the radio of the paramedics. They took our dear friend to the hospital where he passed away on Labor Day. The whole neighborhood seemed to have mixed feelings: First, the happiness we felt for our friend who has gone to his heavenly reward. Second, we felt the grief of his family who loves him so dearly. Third, we felt our own grief at his loss. We'll certainly miss this man we called "The Preacher."

The Preacher was an elderly man who stood tall and erect, and always appeared to have his whole world in total control. This gentle man always had a smile and a friendly *hello* whenever he saw us on the street, or a wave of his hand as we passed in a car.

The Preacher was always very concerned if any of us were having problems; he let us know he didn't wish to interfere but that he was there if we needed him and that he cared about us.

Even tho The Preacher seemed never to have any problems, we all understood how much the troubles of the world concerned him. We knew he maintained his strength by taking all these burdens to the Lord.

The Preacher was a quiet man who, just by walking

amongst us, seemed to radiate God's light. He never had to preach at us; he always shared God's love and strength with us without saying a word.

The Preacher had his reward here on earth too: a lovely wife who loved him dearly. He had the love and respect of all his family and his friends and neighbors.

Even tho we're happy for him now that he's entered God's kingdom, we'll all feel the loss now that he no longer walks bodily amongst us.

We all grew to know and love him, and thru God's love, he'll always walk with us.

We'll miss "The Preacher" — The Rev. Mr. Willingham.

September 4, 1980

A CELEBRATION OF THE CORONATION OF
THE REVEREND W.F. WILLINGHAM

"Thus says the Lord, 'Let not a wise man boast of his wisdom, and let not the mighty man boast of his might, let not a rich man boast of his riches; but let him who boasts of this, that he understands and knows Me, that I am the Lord who exercises loving kindness, justice, and righteousness on earth; for I delight in these things' declares the Lord."
Jeremiah 9:23,24

Prayer   Rev. Lloyd Plunkett
                          Pastor

"Victory in Jesus"   Congregation- led by
                          Rev. Bud Frye

"A Time for Joy"   Carol Wyatt
                          Granddaughter

"Therefore, being always of good courage, and knowing that while we are at home in the body we are absent from the Lord... for we walk by faith, not by sight... we are of good courage, I say, and prefer rather to be absent from the body and to be at home with the Lord. Therefore also we have as our ambition, whether at home or absent, to be pleasing to Him."
II Cor. 5:6-9

"Home, Sweet Home"   Don Willingham
                          Son

Lynn Mayall, son-in-law, and Lin Cravens, nephew, will share in the testimony of his life and the Word.

"You, therefore, my son, be strong in the grace that is in Christ Jesus. And the things which you have heard from me in the presence of many witnesses, these entrust to faithful men, who will be able to teach others also."
II Tim. 2:1,2

"To God Be the Glory"   Congregation

"The Family of God"   Congregation

Your response to the witness of the life of Rev. W.F. Willingham

"Choose ye this day whom you will serve... but as for me and my house, we will serve the Lord."
Joshua 24:15

Graveside Service   Bro Tom Wolf
                          Friend

Victory in Jesus
I heard an old, old story
How a Savior came from glory,
How He gave His Life on Calvary
To save a wretch like me;
I heard about His groaning,
Of His precious blood's a toning
Then I repented of my sins
And won the vicktory.

I heard about a mansion
He has build for me in glory,
And I heard about the streets of gold
Beyond the crystal sea;
About the angels singing,
And the old redemption story,
And some sweet day I'll sing up there
The song of victory.

Chorus on back page

The order of service for Wesley's homegoing celebration.

81

This is the eulogy from the General Baptist Press:

Death Comes To Rev. W. F. Willingham

Brother Wesley Willingham, faithful servant of God and minister to General Baptist Churches for over thirty-five years, died on September 1. Services were held on September 4 in Westminster, California, to celebrate the victory of his life in Christ.

His son-in-law, Lynn Mayall, a pastor in Colorado, and nephew Linuel Cravens, son of Pauline Cravens, led in the praise service. Bud Frye, Executive Secretary of the Sheffield Association, led the congregation, which filled the chapel to overflowing, in singing "Victory in Jesus" and "To God be the Glory." Brother Willingham's son, Don, pastor of the Second General Baptist Church in Dexter, Missouri, sang "My Tribute" and "Home, Sweet Home." Grandsons Doug Willingham and Lance Melton played the piano and organ. Eight grandsons served as pallbearers.

Born in 1902 in Arkansas, the Rev. Willingham had pastored General Baptist Churches in Arkansas, California, and Missouri. He began the church in Willow Springs, Missouri, in 1949. Although he retired from the pastorate at the Ocean View General Baptist Church in Huntington Beach, California, in 1978, he was still actively serving in the First General Baptist Church of Santa Ana. Visiting in homes and hospitals, ministering regularly at a rescue mission, preaching and witnessing whenever an opportunity presented itself was the pattern of his life in retirement.

The supreme goal of his life was to spread the good news of Jesus Christ. God's reconciling work went on at his memorial service as several people accepted Christ as Savior.

He is survived by his wife Deanie, five sons, four daughters, twenty-nine grandchildren, and nine great-grandchildren.

Willingham family reunion in California, 2001.

EPILOGUE

Wesley often used experiences from his life to illustrate spiritual concepts in his sermons. One Sunday Wesley preached a message regarding the incident when Mr. Young blocked the doorway to prevent Mr. Gates from taking Wesley. "Mr. Young stood in my place. He told Mr. Gates, 'To get to Wesley, you have to go through me.' In order to get to God, you have to go through Jesus Christ. He stands in your place. All you have to do is receive Him as your personal Savior."

Have you received Jesus as your Savior? Everyone needs to be saved. All people disobey God's commands, and this sin separates us from a holy God.

As it is written, There is none righteous, no, not one: There is none that understandeth, there is none that seeketh after God. They are all gone out of the way, they are together become unprofitable; there is none that doeth good, no, not one. (Romans 3:10-12)

But after thy hardness and impenitent heart treasurest up unto thyself wrath against the day of wrath

and revelation of the righteous judgment of God.
(Romans 2:5)

The punishment for our sins is death and eternal
separation from God. There is nothing we can do to
earn salvation. God loves us so much that He sent His
only Son, Jesus, to die for our sins. Jesus Christ, who
lived a sinless life, took our place on the cross to pay the
penalty for our sins. Those who accept God's gracious
gift are saved from His wrath.

> For the wages of sin is death; but the gift of God is eter-
> nal life through Jesus Christ our Lord. (Romans 6:23)

> Even the righteousness of God which is by faith of
> Jesus Christ unto all and upon all them that believe:
> for there is no difference: For all have sinned, and come
> short of the glory of God; Being justified freely by his
> grace through the redemption that is in Christ Jesus.
> (Romans 3:22-24)

> But God commendeth his love toward us, in that, while
> we were yet sinners, Christ died for us. Much more
> then, being now justified by his blood, we shall be saved
> from wrath through him. (Romans 5:8-9)

When we accept Jesus as our Savior, God credits
Jesus's righteousness to us.

> For God so loved the world, that he gave his only
> begotten Son, that whosoever believeth in him should
> not perish, but have everlasting life. (John 3:16)

But for us also, to whom it shall be imputed, if we believe on him that raised up Jesus our Lord from the dead; Who was delivered for our offences, and was raised again for our justification. (Romans 4:24-25)

Will you accept Jesus as your Savior today? Wesley's father, William Frank, never stopped looking for his son. In the same way, God loves you so much and is seeking you in order to forgive and save you.

For the Son of man [Jesus Christ] is come to seek and to save that which was lost. (Luke 19:10)

The Lord is not slack concerning his promise, as some men count slackness; but is longsuffering to us-ward, not willing that any should perish, but that all should come to repentance. (2 Peter 3:9)

When Wesley (at six years of age) was walking through the woods to find someone who would give him some food, he had to make a choice when he came to a fork in the trail. He had to decide which way to go. Accepting Jesus as your Savior leads to life — an eternal life in heaven. Rejecting Jesus leads to death and hell. The choice is yours.

For with the heart man believeth unto righteousness; and with the mouth confession is made unto salvation. (Romans 10:10)

For whosoever shall call upon the name of the Lord shall be saved. (Romans 10:13)

Behold, now is the accepted time; behold, now is the day of salvation. (2 Corinthians 6:2)

The Bible says that if you confess with your mouth the Lord Jesus and believe in your heart that God raised him from the dead, you will be saved. If you have not prayed the prayer of salvation and would like to do that now, here is a simple prayer you can pray.

Dear Jesus,

I know I have sinned and rejected you, but now I want to receive you as my Savior. Please forgive me of my sins. I believe in my heart you are the Son of God and you bore my sins on the cross. I know it is by grace that I can be saved, not by anything I can do. I accept you today and will strive to follow you in all I do and say. Your Word says you will dwell in me and guide me. Thank you for being my Savior. I ask this in Jesus Christ's name. Amen.

If you prayed this prayer, you are now a child of God. Find a good Bible-centered church where you can grow in His Word.

APPENDIX A

Transcript of a sermon by Wesley Frank Willingham. Wesley preached this sermon (one of his last messages) at Lynn and Mary Linda's church in Colorado.

What God Won't Do

Well, Ms. Willingham and myself both are just real thrilled to be here tonight. And usually whenever we go back from California to the Midwest and to here, we usually have a revival scheduled somewhere, and we'll pack, I do my — you know most preachers my age — you'll have notebooks, sermons filed away, and so on. And so, I don't know. We didn't think anything about it. I had to cancel a revival that they had wrote me about. I couldn't go, due to the fact of illness. And then whenever I got here, Lynn said, "Now, I announced it that you were going to preach Wednesday night."

And I said, "Well, do you know what I told my church where I belonged? That years ago, if the people of God didn't want me to do anything, not to ask me to." And I feel *that* would be, should be, the way of every Christian.

And I feel highly honored to come here to a lovely building like this, people that love our children and have prayed for them and helped them along life's pathway. And it's our prayer that they'll be a blessing to you, and that you can grow and see the lost brought to Christ.

And whenever he asked me and told me that he had announced it, [he] said, "Would you feel up to it?"

I said, "I never refuse to do anything for the Lord that people ask me to do." A lot of other things.

So it's just our pleasure tonight to be here. And I'll be frank with you. I didn't know what in the world, that a thought, when he mentioned it to me that I'd preach about. So I dreamed about it that night. Now you folks [say], "Why, Old Preacher Willingham, you're kidding." But I'm not! And I want our lesson and message to be tonight on the subject of "What God Won't Do."

Why you say, "I thought He'd do everything." And many people I've heard it said, and I've said it myself that there is nothing too hard for God. But you know there are some things that honestly *God won't do.*

And I want you to open your Bibles tonight to begin with to the 2 Kings, the fifth chapter, and I want us to deal with that lesson and that verse, and then we'll go to Luke 5 and find another lesson in the Word that God didn't, wouldn't deal with a person until this person asked about it, whose heart was right.

Now, I'm not the best reader that you have ever heard of. But you're familiar with it anyhow, and I've read it over and over to the satisfying of myself. And I want us to pray that God will bless in this hour of the message, of this service, whatever the hour may be, hour and a half, or two, or what. But nevertheless, let's pray that God will have His way with all of our hearts here tonight.

Dear Lord, we bow again in your presence to thank you for these people that's here tonight, and this marvelous singing and music that we have heard, and the prayers that's been offered, and the requests for prayers that has been made. Oh, God, how we thank you for it tonight that there is people in our wonderful country that still love you and believe you that you save unto the uttermost, and people that've drifted away can be returned and be restored to fellowship. And we pray as we look into your Word tonight. Will you, as we ask you this afternoon on our knees to come and be the speaker of the hour? Dear Lord, there may be someone here tonight that is doomed for hell without God. And by the way we sing, preach, and pray might be whether or not that this person would be saved or drawn closer to you. Help us to be thankful. And bless as we pray thee through the Holy Spirit of God. In Jesus's name we pray. Amen. Amen.

I don't suppose there's a greater lesson in the Word for us — and we're all familiar with it — and that is this portion of the Word here, where this man was a wonderful person. He was a wonderful man. He had won several wars, and he was high-ranking in his government. But did you know what? He was a leper. And they had taken some people, in fact a maiden from Israel up into their country of Syria, and this little woman, this girl, this little Jewish girl noticed, no doubt that [Naaman had leprosy]. Well, now look. "If my lord (calling Naaman, of course) were down in Israel. There's a prophet down there [that] could really heal him of his leprosy." Now I want us to think that even the government [was concerned for Naaman]. This man was so valuable that he [the king of Syria] would have given anything for him if he could have been healed. Amen? So he wrote a letter. And he said, "You take it to the king of Israel. And whenever he reads it, why, then everything'll be all right, I'm sure." But nevertheless, he takes him some gifts along. And he taken — I believe it was — three or four [ten] raiment of clothes that he made, taken with him to give to the governor, or whoever, that would heal him of this leprosy. But man, this governor [the king of Israel], he got into a rage. He said, "Why, my goodness alive, who thinks that I'm a god that I can heal people. Why, he just wants to start a fight with me, I know." And of course, Elisha heard about it. And I can see him as he sent one of his messengers up, he said, say, "You go up there and tell that feller to come down here. We'll show him that there is a God in Israel."

And this is the responsibility also — allow me to share with you today — that we have in the churches. We need churches, I feel like *you are* that will show Pueblo and the nation today that there's a God in Israel, there's a God in Tamaro that saves souls. Preacher's kids.

A little business that we had in Costa Mesa. I had a habit of witnessing to people that come in. I don't mean from the standpoint that if you have a business that you're to be dogmatic, and I know that some people run people away. But in waiting on this person for whatever that she wanted, I said, "Are you saved? Are you a Christian?"

Why she said, "I sure am. That Methodist preacher down at that Methodist church saved me and my husband too." And she walked out the door.

Well, did you know? Poor thing. She must of — I knew what she meant, of course — but I told someone else there, I said, "Well, bless her heart, she needs help because preachers can't save people." Church members can't save people. People have to let God do for them what they can't do for themselves. And He won't do it unless people are willing for Him to do it. Amen? It's impossible.

And I can see — I don't want to take too much time for this — but I want you to see it. You know I was raised over here in Arkansas. And we went out today to this One-eyed Joe [silversmith shop in Colorado] (whatever you call him out here), where all these old buildings are. Mary Linda and I, we walked right—and it's very fascinating to me—and I told my daughter, I said, "Now these logs were made with a broad ax." A lot of people don't know what a broad ax are, but I did. And I said, "You can see where they chopped 'em out." And I read about where the picture of one where it was moved from some people by the name of Turtle out o' here in the Canyon City, in that area that had homesteaded some ground and made that. I told that lady, I said, "Did you know what? Our forefathers and mothers that blazed a trail before us, brother, they had to have a backbone (that Bud Robinson used to say, "bigger than a mouse's tail"), and also they had to have some stamina. To think what we have here today. This lovely church building. Carpet on the floor. Those people no doubt went to an old log house church, and sat on a board. And I was telling Bro. McClellon there, I was telling him about it. He come tonight. I said, "No doubt, they got happy and shouted the praises of God, because they was filled with the Spirit. They didn't know any better."

For some of us are very smart today, you know. Naaman was smart. I can see him go down to Elisha's house, and I can always imagine that maybe it was a little house maybe like I used to live in Arkansas, made of logs or something. I don't imagine it was a mansion. And I can imagine one of Naaman's servants went in and said, say, "Elisha, did you know there's a great man out here to see you?"

And many of us, we would say, "Yeah!" And here we would have bursted out to see him, shook hands with him, and [said], "How in the world are you doing, Naaman?"

But Elisha sent his servant out, said, "You go tell him,

go down to the Jordan and bathe seven times, and he'll be clean.

Naaman said, "I thought surely he would come out and maybe run his hand over me or something or other, at least honor me and tell me that now your leprosy is gone. But I'm not going to do *that*."

You see honestly, our thought and lesson is God won't do something for people that they can do themselves. You can't save yourself, but you have to be willing to be saved. You can't be a church like God wants, but you have to be willing, brother. Then God will use you.

But you know the story, don't you? Finally, Naaman, in a rage he left, but they said, "Naaman, if he had asked you to give him a great amount of money, you'd have give it to him. If he'd asked you to give him your gifts, you would have. And here you are going back." And he said, "You better go back down there and bathe in that river."

And you can see the point. Naaman couldn't get rid of his leprosy, but whenever he was obedient to God, whenever he was obedient, then his leprosy was gone. Then he runs back up and wants to give Elisha something for it. And he told him, "Oh, no. Not as I live, as I breathe, you go right ahead." He didn't take it.

In the fifth chapter of the book of Luke, secondly, we find God won't strengthen and help businesses of Christian people until they are obedient to God. You know, here was a fisherman, and they fished at night. If you'll notice verse two, that Luke said here, "And [Jesus] saw two ships here standing by the lake. But the fishermen were gone out then and were washing their nets. And he entered into one of the ships, which was Simon's, and prayed him that he would thrust out a little ways." And as he did, he stopped, and Jesus spoke to the multitude on the shores. Then whenever He had finished speaking, He told Peter, He said, "Peter," said, "Launch out into the deep."

Peter's reply was — you'll find it here. And Simon answered and said (in verse five), said, "Master, we have toiled all night, and we haven't caught anything or taken anything."

Now isn't that about like us? Amen? Many a time, it's just about like us. He was just human. Like you and I. But I want you to notice though he said here, but he said, "We've toiled all night and have taken nothing. Nevertheless," he said, "at thy will, I will let down the net." Oh, what a message, and what a thought. You see, whenever he was obedient to God. God could have put the fish in the net, I'm confident, without him a-letting it down. But there was something for him to do.

I'm reminded — if you don't mind for me to share it with you — and sometimes this makes me think [of] a Sunday school teacher of a church that Ms. Willingham and I were serving when Mary was very little, very small. One day, Mary was saved, and I shall never forget it — but that wasn't what I was going to say — but when the people were coming by and shaking hands with her. She just came to the altar because Ms. Willingham came with someone else.

She told me going home, she said, "Daddy," said, "did no one shake hands with *me*."

Well I said, "Sweetheart, did you take Christ as your Savior?"

She said, "I sure did."

I said, "We will tonight."

But nevertheless, the lady that I started to tell you about, in this same church, her husband was a carpenter. He directed the choir, and he also was a deacon in the church and a Sunday school teacher. Whenever she got to have one car (and of course he used it going to his work), and whenever she wanted to go to town, downtown, she'd call a taxi.

And I was proddin' the people along, I said, "Now let's work and see if God don't give us souls, and let's pray that souls will be saved."

And she invited this taxi driver to come, and he come. Twice. And he didn't come back. Well, I didn't—you know, it was pretty good size, a pretty good group—and I didn't know why. I didn't even know he'd ever come. Sorry to say. But I didn't. But anyhow, she called a day or two, needed to go to town. And she called, and the man came and taken her to town, and said, "Say," when she got out, she said, "We didn't see you at church last Sunday."

"Oh," he said. "No," said, "I like your singing and everything, but," he said, "it was good, but," said, "I couldn't stand your preacher."

Well she said, "What's the matter with our preacher?"

Listen. "Well," he said, "he makes cold chills run up and down my back."

I said, "Sister [Lea?], you tell that taxi driver that that wasn't your big old preacher, but it was God." It was God wanting that person to do something. He wanted him to yield to something. He wanted him to obey to the invitation. Couldn't save himself.

This businessman, Peter, here said, "Lord, we've toiled all night." And let me tell you something. They fished in the night. Unusual for them probably to go fishing in the daytime. They were washing their nets, and I can imagine that Peter would say, "Well, I'm tired. I'm ready to go home." But he said, "As *you* said."

Now I want you to notice something else. That their

nets were so full that he hollered for someone else to come and help him. And do you know what? There is never no one that I ever know in my life that was saved but what they didn't want to see someone else saved. Amen? It's just something or other that we can't retain. It's something or other that is so good that we want to share it with someone else.

And so he called, "Come, you folks, and help us here." He said, "We've got more than we can handle." They couldn't. They'd toiled all night. And they was good fishermen. But when God spoke and they were obedient, their nets was full.

Thirdly and lastly — and I'm not as young as I used to be — (and probably you wouldn't want me to preach very long anyhow), but I want you to look at John 11. And we want to fill you with this portion of the Word. In John 11, he said here, "Now a certain man was sick, which was Lazarus," — as you know — "and he lived in Bethany in a town of Mary and her sister Martha. (And it was that Mary which anointed the Lord with ointment and wiped his feet with the hair of her head, whose brother Lazarus was sick.) Therefore, his sisters sent unto him, saying, 'Lord, behold, he whom thou lovest is sick.'"

Now you know that — and I want to drop down into verse 40. You know that Jesus didn't go (especially you that teach Sunday school and you that have studied your Bible), and Jesus had a purpose of not going. And He didn't go.

But I want you to notice. Let's take up verse 38, at least, and he said, "Jesus therefore again groaning," that is after he had come now to the tomb. "After that He was standing by the grave, and it was a cave, and a stone lay upon it. And Jesus said, 'Take ye away the stone.' Martha, the sister of him that was dead said unto him,

'Lord, by this time, he stinketh, because he had been dead four days.' "

Now the thought and the lesson tonight is that God won't do some things. He didn't roll the stone away. And I was telling Lynn, and I was thinking, and I didn't know it, but as I read verse 41, I'm convinced that somebody helped Martha roll that stone away. And this told me something or other that one person can't have a church by himself. Amen? It takes all, everybody. Not only the staff of a church, but it takes people like you that are here. And some of you may be here for the first time. But whatever you may be. But let me tell you something. You're just as important as anyone. Don't let nobody tell you, because you're not a deacon or an usher, or because you're not the pastor, or because you're not the choir director or the educational teacher or minister. Brother, let me tell you something. You're just as important as any. God loves you, and He died for you. And He wants to save you. He wants you to let Him save you if you're here and lost.

Every Wednesday night, I go to a rescue mission—every fourth Wednesday night (sorry). Here sometime back, I got out of my car and had my Bible in my hand, and there was people all around there, and there was dope, and they was smoking, and they was drunk and this and that in this rescue mission, waiting for the service, and then they was going to eat. And it's always full. But they didn't come to hear me preach. Brother, they come to get something to eat. I got out of my car, and a lamppost there was on the sidewalk.

An old boy come up to me, and he staggered around, and he said, "Say, are you going to preach here tonight?"

I said, "Well, Lord willing, I am."

He said, "Would you pray for me?"

I said, "I sure will. Will you pray for me?"

Well, he said, "I need you to pray for *me*."

I said, "Well, let's pray right here at this lamppost."

All these other fellows, you know how it is in town in Santa Ana, California. It's a pretty good-sized place.

And so, I said, "You pray first."

And he said, "Sandy" (that's his wife's name). Said, "You know I'm sorry that I left you. I wish I was at home, Sandy."

And I tell you never heard such a prayer. After he prayed, I prayed. And now I don't say this other than that I just give God the glory for it. Every night, there've been anywhere from nine to twelve men, and sometimes women, come forward, kneel at an old-fashion altar and pray to take Jesus as their Savior. And you know why? I tell them they don't have to be in that stupor. They don't have to be like that. God wants to save them and make something out of them.

The man that always leads the singing, he come to me—almost a year ago now—and he said, "I want to tell you something, Bro. Wesley." Said, "I sure appreciate what you tell those men." Said, "You tell them God loves them." Said, "I have been here where preachers that scolded them all the time, because that they were drunk, and the stupor that they were in."

And certainly I guess they needed it. But you know there was a time, whenever they needed something that God had for them, but they have to be where that they'll let God do it for them. Amen?

And here we see a great miracle. I want you to notice that in the doubts though, however, in Martha. And you notice what Jesus told her. (We'll close in a little bit.) "When he had heard therefore that he was sick." (Wait, I'm reading in the wrong place. I'm sorry.) "But Jesus said unto her, 'Said I not' (notice in verse 40) 'unto thee, that, if thou wouldest believe, thou shouldest see the glory of God?' " Mary, Martha. I told you that you would.

And you know, they had some other men, I believe. I believe I'm right in this, because in verse 41, if you'll notice now, he said, "and *they* took away the stone from the place where the dead was laid. And Jesus lifted up his eyes toward heaven and said, 'Father, I thank thee.'"

Praise God tonight for the old-time, Holy Ghost, God said, Baptist religion, salvation that saves people, and they know it. "He said, 'I thank thee because thou hast heard me. There are those that stand by. Lord, here I am, and for that reason.' He cried with a loud voice, and He said, 'Lazarus, come forth.'"

Now I want you to notice something else. He could have rolled the stone away, but He didn't. What else? See this man as he stands there with grave clothes on. And you know what else? He could have taken the grave clothes off of him, but He didn't. He said, "Loose him, and let him go."

Oh, my good Christian people tonight, Lord help me, and let's help each other to thank God that God has a purpose in life for every person.

You'll notice in Matthew 11 in verses 28 and 29. Here again. You know as you — especially as I do — I can visualize, and I can imagine things. Sometimes I don't know if they were that way or not, but I know one thing. That there was Sadducees, Pharisees, strict law-livers in Jesus's day. And I've always thought. (And this is just my own personal thinking. It may not be true at all.) But I always thought, after I have read this, that maybe Jesus was sitting upon the Mount of Olives, and maybe that He looked down upon some of those people that He had prayed for and loved, and some of them maybe had witnessed raising of the dead, opening the eyes of the blind. And then I could imagine that he could see going along here was an old yoke of oxen, you know with a yoke upon their neck, and calluses like we used to [get] on the farm, where people that farmed and their mules would have calluses, maybe on their necks or something. Some of you know what I'm talking about, don't you? Amen? And I can imagine *that*, because of what He said. I imagine He looked to them under the law, and what a burden it was that had been put upon them.

Notice (in closing) that He said now, something like this, said, "Come unto me all ye that labor and are heavy laden." Couldn't you imagine an ol' yoke of an ox on his neck would get very heavy, pulling the load, with the laden behind him. And He said, "I'll give you rest." But notice, He asked him to come. He didn't tell him He'd give it to him without coming. And He said, "Take my yoke upon ye, and learn of me; for I am meek and lowly in heart: and you shall find rest unto your souls."

I can imagine this is why Jesus was motivated to say what He said. And you know why, this is why I'm a Baptist. First of all, this is why I'm saved. First of all, I believe that, people, you must be born again. And then I believe in a Bible-believing, Bible-preaching church. People oughta find 'em one. And I believe you oughta be a member of it. And He said, "My yoke." (Am I wrong in my thinking?) Verse 30. And He said, "My yoke is easy. My burden is light."

Yes. God wants to save everybody that's lost. But He can't save a person unless that person is willing to be saved. There may be those, and oft times I have shared this with people that have cried even, and tears in their eyes [said,] "I know, I know, preacher, I'm not living where I ought to be. I'm not doing what I ought to do for God. And I know I should. But someway or another, I just can't."

Young man told me one time (that was saved at one of our meetings), and he was a young fellow, and I said — well, 'bout ten or twelve years old — and I said, "Son, do you want to unite with the church and be baptized?"

He said, "Yes, I do."

I said, "Would you let me and the bus minister go to your home and talk to your mother and father?"

We did. We prayed with them. I said, "Would you help him spiritually and your children? He wants to be baptized. He presented himself to the church."

"Oh," she said, "Bro. Willingham, we sure will."

And you know what that little fellow told me? The next Sunday, I was out, there was a water fountain out in front of the church. And here he just got off the bus, and he's come going in, and he stopped, and he said, "Bro. Willingham," said, "my mother said I didn't have to be baptized."

I said, "Your mother's right. You don't even have to be saved. But we as a church, if we teach you and learn as we should of Jesus, you should be obedient."

He said, "Can you prove it to me?"

I said, "I can read it to you out of the Word." And I turned there on the steps — somewhere maybe similar to yours up here, maybe not quite as big — and read it to him.

He looked up to me, and he said, "Bro. Willingham, I want to be baptized."

Here's what Jesus said. You see, you may be here tonight, and there may be a great victory for you if you'd let Jesus give it to you. But you have to be willing to let Him. You may be lost. You may have sin in your life, and you've never confessed it. And you may be lost and doomed for hell without God. But you say, "I want to be saved." But you'll never be saved. God will never save you against your will. You'll have to be a John 1:12. He said, "as many as received him, to them gave he power to become the sons of God, to them that he gave them power that they wanted to be."

I want us to have prayer. This is prayer meeting night. I want you to bow your heads and your hearts with me. And I want you that are Christians, and you know that you're saved. God loves you, and I love you. And I'm not up here just to be a-preaching. We come on a vacation, but if I can help somebody to know Jesus, I'd leave, go back happy. While heads are bowed and eyes are closed, and no one looking around, every one of you that know that you're saved and beyond a shadow of a doubt that you're saved, would you raise your hand and say, "I know I'm saved. I let Jesus do for me what I couldn't do for myself." Amen. God bless you. God bless you.

While heads are bowed and eyes are closed and Christians are praying, I want to pray. And I want to pray for you. But before we pray, is there someone here that didn't raise your hand awhile ago, if you'd be honest, and say, "Bro. Willingham, I'm sorry. I just couldn't. But I know my heart is not right with God. I'm far from God." The devil may be saying, "You've never been here before." But that don't make any difference. The Lord loves you, and He wants to save you. "I don't have no church home, but I need one, I want one." Anyone? You'd raise your hand before we pray and say, "Remember me. I want God to save me. I can't save myself." Anyone? While we wait. Before we pray. Raise your hand and say, "Pray for me." Anyone? Anywhere? While Christians are praying. You can roll that stone away. Jesus would. If you just roll it away, He'd come in. If you're here tonight, I want you to stand with us for prayer, please.

> Our Father, we bow before you to thank you for the Word of God, and as we've looked here into your Word, and we've seen great renown men that saw their need for God, for things that they couldn't do, and that God wouldn't save them without them being obedient. Father, if there is a person here tonight that honestly would be honest with himself and say, "Preacher Willingham, I need help tonight. I want the church to pray for me. And I want to be saved — whatever it is." We pray in Jesus's name tonight that the Holy Spirit will do His office work, and He'll do things right now that they'll be glad that they done even a hundred years from now, if they should live that long. Give us strength, we pray. And bless and save souls. In Jesus's name we pray. Amen

CPSIA information can be obtained
at www.ICGtesting.com
Printed in the USA
BVHW051227060323
659771BV00009B/413